Online Anti-Semitism in Turkey

DOI: 10.1057/9781137507945.0001

Other Palgrave Pivot titles

palgrave▶pivot

Online Anti-Semitism in Turkey

Türkay Salim Nefes

Research Associate, University of Oxford, UK

palgrave
macmillan

DOI: 10.1057/9781137507945.0001

First published in 2015 by
PALGRAVE MACMILLAN®
in the United States—a division of St. Martin's Press LLC,
175 Fifth Avenue, New York, NY 10010.

Where this book is distributed in the UK, Europe and the rest of the world,
this is by Palgrave Macmillan, a division of Macmillan Publishers Limited,
registered in England, company number 785998, of Houndmills,
Basingstoke, Hampshire RG21 6XS.

Palgrave Macmillan is the global academic imprint of the above companies
and has companies and representatives throughout the world.

Palgrave® and Macmillan® are registered trademarks in the United States,
the United Kingdom, Europe and other countries.

ISBN: 978–1–137–50795–2 EPUB
ISBN: 978–1–137–50794–5 PDF
ISBN: 978–1–137–50796–9 Hardback

Library of Congress Cataloging-in-Publication Data is available from
the Library of Congress.

A catalogue record of the book is available from the British Library.

First edition: 2015

www.palgrave.com/pivot

DOI: 10.1057/9781137507945

This book is dedicated to the memory of Hayriye Ozcelik and Salim Nefes

DOI: 10.1057/9781137507945.0001

Contents

DOI: 10.1057/9781137507945.0001

List of Tables

Acknowledgements

This study was made possible by a generous grant from the Vidal Sassoon International Center for the Study of Antisemitism. I would like to acknowledge my gratitude to the centre for this support. I would also like to thank the Sociology Department at the University of Oxford for being great hosts to the research. In particular, my overall research benefited a lot from the mentorship of Dr Michael Biggs. I wrote the final version of this book during my research stay at the Conspiracy and Democracy project in the Centre for Research in the Arts, Social Sciences and Humanities, University of Cambridge. The book benefited a great deal from their hospitality. The help of Tulay Nefes, Carlos Iborra and Maria Jose Maza eased the process of writing the book. I would also like to thank my wife, Alexandra Iborra Maza and son Elias Nefes Iborra, for their support and patience. Last but not the least, the assistant editor Lani Oshima and publisher Mireille Yanow were very helpful in the production process of this book.

DOI: 10.1057/9781137507945.0003

Introduction

Abstract: *This chapter initially unveils the subject main of this study, online anti-Semitism in contemporary Turkey, and explains its significance. Then, it explains methodological and theoretical approaches of the research and contextualizes the study in the academic literature. Lastly, it outlines the plan of the book.*

Nefes, Türkay Salim. *Online Anti-Semitism in Turkey.* New York: Palgrave Macmillan, 2015. DOI: 10.1057/9781137507945.0004.

▶

While official accounts in Turkey highlight the Turkish tolerance towards non-Muslims, the popularity of anti-Semitic books, such as *Mein Kampf*, in the 2000s (Nefes, 2012, 2013a, 2015) raise doubts about this picture. Moreover, the recent political tension between Israel and Turkey is likely to have repercussions on the perception and experience of Turkish Jewry. PEW survey data (2015) demonstrates a steeply increasing trend of anti-Jewish feelings in Turkey over recent years: it shows that very unfavourable views about Jews have steadily increased from 32% to 69% between 2004 and 2011. In addition, a recent study on hate speech in Turkish mainstream media suggests that Jews were the group that were most frequently the subject of hate speech between May and September 2014: the research classified 130 articles as hate speech about Jews and 60 articles as hate speech against Armenians (Dink Foundation, 2015). In short, recent socio-political changes since 2000 during AKP rule, attested in the popular term 'new' Turkey, render the Jewish minority experience a very important but insufficiently explored area of research that could enlighten the new phase of Muslim–Jewish relations in Turkey.

This book fills this scholarly lacuna by being the first study that focuses on online anti-Semitism in Turkey. The research mainly relies on the content analysis of comments about Adolf Hitler in the most popular Turkish forum website, Ekşi Sözlük, between 1999 and 2013. This is preceded by a discussion of major historical events concerning Turkish Jewry that gives a brief historical account about the Jewish experience in Turkey. The book intends to unveil the current perception of the Jewish identity and the ways in which anti-Semitic themes are discussed by affording information about the communication of anti-Semitism in everyday conversations. Before going further, it should be stated that the research defines anti-Semitism as hostility toward Jews as a religious group or race. It is in line with Klug's (2003) description of the term as a view that portrays Jews as 'an alien presence, a parasite that preys on humanity and seeks to dominate the world. Across the globe, their hidden hand controls the banks, the markets and the media...'

This introductory chapter explains theoretical and methodological perspectives briefly and then outlines relevant academic literatures on Turkish anti-Semitism, online political communication and racism. Last, it provides a brief outline of the book.

DOI: 10.1057/9781137507945.0004

Theoretical perspective

This research makes use of rational choice theory in its attempt to delineate and analyse anti-Semitism in online discussions. The basic reason behind this choice is that rational choice theory attempts to understand the logic behind people's actions. Coleman (1990: 17–18) points to that in the following manner: '...much of what is ordinarily described as non-rational or irrational is merely so because the observers have not discovered the point of view of the actor, from which the action *is* rational.' As this study's emphasis is on giving meaning to people's contributions to an online discussion, rational choice theory's focus on analysing individual's logic and action fits the research's purposes. For example, Nefes (2014b) used rational choice perspective effectively to understand the rationales of online users in proposing conspiracy theories about an attempted assassination in Taiwan. He found that online users propose conspiracy theories in line with their political cost-benefit considerations and perceived threats.

Rational choice theory assists this work in delineating online users' rationales by examining their entries both from cost-benefit and moral points of view. First, in line with classical rational choice perspective, it examines the ways in which people use instrumental rationale in those conversations. For example, while analysing people's entries about Adolf Hitler, the study underlines negative and positive material aspects of Hitler that online users propose, such as being a good military commander, his ability to convince masses or his lack of comprehension of modern warfare. Second, in line with Boudon's (1996, 2001, 2003, 2008) cognitivist theory of action, a variant of rational choice perspective that refers to values and beliefs or statements other than consequential instrumental type, the study explores values that online users highlight in their conversations. The study underscores what kind of values people use in their descriptions of Adolf Hitler, such as evil or hero.

Using rational choice theory enables the study to take into account both value-laden and rationalistic aspects of online users' views and provide a comprehensive account. This is particularly fruitful in differentiating positive instrumental/material comments from anti-Semitic remarks. For example, many people might see a military genius in Hitler by thinking that he was a great commander winning many wars. This is a positive instrumental comment, but it does not have to be classified as anti-Semitic, because it does not involve a moral evaluation of

DOI: 10.1057/9781137507945.0004

Jewish people. However, if the comment portrays Hitler as a morally right person with regards to the Holocaust, then it is clearly anti-Semitic, because it involves a positive moral judgement about a major anti-Semitic catastrophe. In this way, the study is able to probe the perception of Jews in 'new' Turkey and provide an astute analysis.

Methods

The research mainly relies on content analysis of conversations about Adolf Hitler to explore the ways in which anti-Semitic themes are interpreted and communicated by Turkish people. Hitler, like the Holocaust (Alexander, 2009), is a historically significant theme in anti-Semitism globally, representing moral evil and human suffering. Hitler's book, *Mein Kampf*, was a bestseller in the Turkish book market in 2005, which seems to suggest that there was an interest in his ideas (Bali, 2009; Smith, 2005). This could be a symptom of an increase in anti-Semitism in Turkish society. The e-book version of *Mein Kampf* was in second place on Amazon's political science and ideology bestseller list in the United Kingdom (Flood, 2014). Chris Faraone, an author, suggests that the current popularity of *Mein Kampf* in e-book format is because the electronic format enables people to read the book in private without having to demonstrate it on their bookshelves or while travelling: 'People might not have wanted to buy *Mein Kampf* at Borders or have it delivered to their home or displayed on their living room bookshelf, let alone get spotted reading it on a subway, but judging by hundreds of customer comments online, readers like that digital copies can be quietly perused then dropped into a folder or deleted' (Flood, 2014). In the Turkish case, the popularity of *Mein Kampf* could also be due to the fact that there are not any norms against reading it. Examining the ways in which the word Hitler was used by Turkish online users provides valuable evidence on anti-Semitism in Turkey on an everyday level.

Scholarship on online political communication

As this study explores the political communication related to online perception of Adolf Hitler and anti-Semitism in Turkey, the scholarship

DOI: 10.1057/9781137507945.0004

on online racism and political deliberations is of imperative relevance to the discussion. The academic literature labels the Internet as a new venue for the creation and confirmation of identities (Byrne, 2008; Castells, 1997; Ignacio, 2005; Nakamura, 2002; Turkle, 1997). While some studies demonstrate that websites can function as a venue where experiences about marginalization and racism can be shared and challenged (Parker and Song, 2009), many others describe the Internet as a new medium for racism today (Adams and Roscigno, 2005; Daniels, 2009a, 2009b; Douglas et al., 2005; McNamee et al., 2010; Perry and Olsson, 2009; Picca and Feagin, 2007; Steinfeldt et al., 2010; Wojcieszak, 2010). Back (2002) underlines that the Internet affords a new space for white racist culture to flourish. Daniels (2009a) explores the reasons and impacts of the spread of racism online and analyses the dissemination and perception of white supremacy. Most of these studies have their geographical focus on the United States (Douglas et al., 2005). There are not any studies on online hatred and racism in Turkey to date. This book fills this gap and builds on the scholarly debates by focusing on the comments about Adolf Hitler in an Internet forum. It scrutinizes the ways in which Hitler is perceived by online users to delineate the anti-Semitic mindset and its alternatives. In so doing, it also engages with the questions that concerned this literature: to what extent does the forum website function for the affirmation of anti-Semitic sentiments? How do people rationalize or challenge the anti-Semitic ideas surrounding the image of Adolf Hitler on the Internet? Does the Internet function as a vanguard against contemporary racism or solely as a conduit of it?

Another relevant debate in the scholarship on online political communication is about people's engagement with opinion-challenging views. Various studies underline that the Internet increases political fragmentation, as people tend to look for and contribute to the political views and information that are in line with theirs and avoid the ones that contradict their pre-existing ideas (Adamic and Glance, 2005; Bimber and Davis, 2003; Himelboim et al., 2013; Iyengar and Hahn, 2009; Johnson et al., 2009; Sunstein, 2001). Parmelee and Bichard (2011) found that people are more likely to be influenced by the politicians on Twitter with whom they ideologically agree, more often than the ones with whom they ideologically disagree. Sunstein (2001) warns that the tendency to selective exposure to online political content is harmful for democratic deliberation. However, other studies question the selective political exposure

DOI: 10.1057/9781137507945.0004

on the Internet thesis by claiming that people do not exhibit a systematic bias against opinion-challenging information (Garrett, 2009). Yardi and Boyd (2010) take a middle stance with their evidence for people's online engagement with opinion-challenging and opinion-reinforcing political content in online discussions about abortion. This discussion might imply that political debates in non-political forums, to which people will not be biased to join, could be places where democratic debates between contrasting views take place online. Indeed, Wojcieszak and Mutz (2009) found that many non-political online forums were used for political discussions and facilitated an exchange of contradictory opinions. In that regard, Ekşi Sözlük provides an ideal venue for investigating online political discussions by being both a non-political and popular forum website in Turkey. By focusing on the content of an online discussion on Adolf Hitler in Ekşi Sözlük and showing to what extent the discussion involves contrasting views, this study affords fresh evidence to this debate from an unexplored context.

Academic literature on Turkish anti-Semitism

Aside from the scholarship on online political communication, this study builds on previous studies on Turkish Jewry and anti-Semitism. We could divide the literature on Turkish anti-Semitism into two major views: (a) Turkish society provides a tolerant and welcoming atmosphere for Jews. Anti-Semitism has never existed as a mainstream current neither in modern Turkey nor during its predecessor the Ottoman Empire. Turkish anti-Semitism is only confined to marginal groups and cultural stereotypes, prejudices, rumours, and conspiracy theories (Alkan, 2000; Kuyaş, 2009; Levy, 1994; Shaw, 1991; Toktaş, 2006); (b) Jews are not treated equally as Turkish citizens, and anti-Semitism is an everyday phenomenon born out of insecurities about the loyalty of non-Muslim minorities in Turkey (Bali, 2001, 2004, 2006, 2009; Brink-Danan, 2009, 2010, 2011, 2012). Below, the study discusses these two views in detail.

a. Hospitable Turks and grateful Jews

Shaw's (1991) *The Jews of the Ottoman Empire and the Turkish Republic* is emblematic to the view that sees anti-Semitism as a fringe aspect of Turkish culture and politics. Shaw (1991) recounts the story of Jews in the Ottoman Empire and the Turkish Republic, presenting both as

DOI: 10.1057/9781137507945.0004

welcoming hosts that protected the Jewish community and allowed it to flourish, and the Jewish community as loyal subjects who served the country well. Some examples of that are as follows: Sultan Bayazid II issued a formal invitation to the Jews expelled from Spain in the fifteenth century (Shaw, 1991: 40); Sultan Abdul Mecid issued an order, *ferman*, on 6 November 1840 to absolve Ottoman Jewry of guilt in blood libel accusations and assured that in such cases the Ottoman court would investigate the claims and provide justice (Shaw, 1991: 200); Sultan Abdulhamid II rejected Theodor Herzl's request in 1901 to create a Jewish settlement in Palestine, but welcomed persecuted Jews to all throughout the empire not solely to Palestine (Shaw, 1991: 212–213); during the Second World War, Turkey did not submit to Nazi pressure to turn over Jewish refugees, and provided a passage for them to flee from Nazi persecution (Shaw, 1991: 256–257). In this picture, most of the anti-Semitic incidents were attributed to the Christian minorities in the Ottoman period, especially Greeks and Armenians who competed with the Jewish community and then to marginal Islamist and international terrorist groups during the Turkish Republic. For example, Shaw (1991: 269) mentions that the praise of Hitler for the elimination of Jews by an Islamist politician, İbrahim Halil Çelik, did not create an anti-Semitic surge and was criticized both by Turkish and Jewish leaders.

Shaw (1991) underlines the loyalty, assimilation and help of the Jewish community in Turkey. He remarks that the Ottoman Empire and the Jews had a shared fate and both progressed and declined together (Shaw, 1991: 121). He notes that the Jewish population has increasingly been using Turkish as a native language since the establishment of the Turkish Republic, which is replacing the Judeo-Spanish of the older generations, also known as Ladino (Shaw, 1991: 265–266). He adds that as a result of the equality of opportunity provided to Turkish Jews, they are assimilating. Their native language is Turkish, and they go to Turkish schools with Muslim Turks: 'Some Turkish Jews have either become Muslims or have entirely abandoned religion in order to become part of the secular way of life established in Turkey' (Shaw, 1991: 267). Shaw (1991) mentions that the establishment of the state of Israel created strains in relations between Turkish Muslims and Jews, and emigration to Israel left the older generations in Turkey. Moreover, Turkish state secularism restricted the actions of Jewish foundations as well as Muslim foundations (Shaw, 1991: 268–269). Overall, Shaw's positive description of Turkish Jewry fits well with the occasion of the

DOI: 10.1057/9781137507945.0004

year 1992, when the symbolic 500th year of Jewish existence in Turkey was celebrated:

> Despite the problems, then, Turkish Jewry remains extremely comfortable, secure in its Turkish patriotism, strongly loyal to the Turkish Republic, and extremely resentful of outside non-Jewish nationalist groups that have tried to disturb the relationship for their own purposes by claiming that Turkish Jewry is being persecuted to attract the support for world Jewry for their national causes. The recent offer by the King of Spain to allow Sephardic Jews to return to Spain and resume their Spanish citizenship after a five hundred year exile has been taken up by no one in Turkey or elsewhere. Emigration to Israel by Turkish Jews has virtually come to an end, with the few still going doing so largely because of considerations of greater economic opportunities for private commercial enterprise rather than any sort of feelings of persecution or prejudice in Turkey. (Shaw, 1991: 270)

In parallel, Galante (1947) earlier highlighted the Turkish hospitality towards the Jewish minority and Turkish Jewry's patriotism in his historical analysis. Indeed, Shaw's (1991) work could be seen as a more comprehensive and updated account of Galanti's book. Echoing the perspectives of these studies, Kuyaş (2009: 53) claims that anti-Semitic tradition neither exists in Islam nor in the Ottoman Empire, and Turkey continues in the same tradition, not imitating Western anti-Semitism. However, he reminds us that modern citizenship has not instituted itself in Turkey yet, and when there was relevant political conjuncture and provocations, masses turned against the Jews. Tackling the same question, Toktaş (2006) interviewed Turkish Jews about the treatment of the community in Turkey. The respondents claimed that an ordinary Turkish citizen in Anatolia would not know who a Jew is or what is Judaism, but would have some knowledge about non-Muslims, just enough to differentiate them from Muslims. They added that anti-Semitism in Turkey is very weak compared to Europe (Toktaş, 2006: 212). Toktaş's findings suggest that anti-Semitism in Turkey is infrequent and happening on an individual level, prejudices that are not reflected in political movements. The Turkish Jews afforded a positive picture about their status in Turkey and did not feel threatened by anti-Semitism except the marginal cases of Islamist media: 'The scope of anti-Semitism remained limited to negative stereotypes about Jews, and provocations of Islamists, fed by the impact of the Israel–Palestine conflict' (Toktaş, 2006: 220).

Contrastingly, in a previous study, Toktaş (2005) gives a historical analysis of the political treatment of the Jews in the Turkish Republic

DOI: 10.1057/9781137507945.0004

and underlines the state policy to undermine the power of the Chief Rabbinate, the 'Citizen, Speak Turkish' campaign, stereotypes about Jews in Turkish media, anti-Semitic attacks in Thrace in the 1940s, the Incident of Reserves during the Second World War, and the September 6–7 events in 1957. Toktaş (2005: 421) proposes that the Jewish population was generally perceived as a loyal community in Turkish politics, as they did not take part in the independence movements that dismembered the Ottoman Empire and played roles in denying the accusations about the Armenian genocide. However, this was not sufficient for the state to consider them as Turks. Toktaş (2005: 421–422) suggests that strong secularism in Turkey that restricted religion to the private sphere played a double role for the community. On the one hand, it curbed down their religious freedom. On the other hand, the staunch secularist ideology prevented the flourishing of Islamic fundamentalism and therefore provided a safe haven for the Jewish minority.

Lewis (1984) provides a wider historical perspective on potential reasons for the Turkish tolerance in his book, *The Jews of Islam*. Lewis (1984) claims that Muslim societies gave more freedom to Jews compared to Christian countries, especially until the nineteenth century. According to Lewis (1984), one of the main reasons for this is Islam's recognition of all other Abrahamic religions, Christianity and Judaism. While Jews were given the status of a believer, they were not considered equal to Muslims who follow 'the finest and most perfect religion' (Shaw, 1991: 9). Therefore, there were not religious-based conflicts between Muslims and the other followers of the Abrahamic faiths like the tension between Christianity and Judaism: 'In Islamic society hostility to the Jew is non-theological... For Muslims, it is not part of the birth pangs of their religion, as it is for Christians. It is rather the usual attitude of the dominant to the subordinate' (Lewis, 1984: 85). This is also evident in blood libel accusations, which was mainly spread by and among Christian populations. There was a relatively peaceful relationship between Jews and Muslims:

> All this helped to create, in earlier though not later Islamic times, a kind of symbiosis between Jews and their neighbours that has no parallel in the Western world between the Hellenistic and modern ages. Jews and Muslims had extensive and intimate contacts that involved social as well as intellectual association—cooperation, commingling, even personal friendship. (Lewis, 1984: 88)

DOI: 10.1057/9781137507945.0004

Accordingly, the Turkish attitude towards the Jewish minority was predominantly shaped by tolerance alloyed with contempt for not following the finest religion: 'Even when the Turkish attitude toward Jews was negative, it was on the whole contemptuous rather than hostile, and it does not seem to have caused any noticeable inconvenience to Jews until the seventeenth century and after' (Lewis, 1984: 138). Moreover, Ottomans considered the Jewish minority as an economically useful and productive community. Although providing a positive picture about the Ottoman/Turkish tolerance, Lewis (1984: 138) disagrees with the view that Ottomans unconditionally opened their borders to the expelled Jews from Spain and Portugal in the fifteenth century. He claims that the Jews were led to and sometimes forced to settle in selected places that the Ottoman authorities thought as suitable.

Common themes proposed in the optimistic vision of Turkish Jewry can be summarized as follows:

(a) Turks welcomed and protected the persecuted Jewish populations throughout history.
(b) Jews were loyal citizens of the Ottoman Empire and Turkey, and they contributed immensely to the development of their country.
(c) In Turkey and the Ottoman Empire, anti-Semitic movements did not emerge from mainstream Turkish society. They were either other minorities, such as Greeks and Armenians, or marginal political movements, such as radical Islamists, or individual cases that cannot be generalized.

Although these studies portray a peaceful relationship between the Jewish minority and Turkish society, there is an intrinsic understanding that the Jews are grateful guests and Turks are the hospitable host. It implies that the Jews are not full members of the Turkish nation, but very loyal and useful non-local residents. Moreover, we do not know what to make of Lewis' (1984) view of Islamic tolerance towards Jews in secular Turkish society, where the importance of religion in public life has gradually declined.

b. Turkish Jews as outsiders

Bali (2001, 2004, 2006, 2009), Brink-Danan (2012) and other scholars (Baer, 2006, 2013; Haker, 2003; Içduygu et al., 2008; Nefes, 2012, 2013a, 2014a, 2015) illustrate the negative view with regards to perception of the

Jewish minority in Turkey with historical and ethnographic evidence using examples such as the Wealth Tax in 1942 that imposed a heavy levy on all non-Muslims in Turkey. They criticized the opposite view for advocating a false, happy minority image serving the Turkish state ideology.

Içduygu et al. (2008) studied the emigration patterns of non-Muslim minorities from Turkey, namely Armenians, Jews and Greeks. They note that the population of the non-Muslim minorities in Turkey has gradually declined from around three per cent to less than one per thousand since the establishment of the Turkish Republic in the 1920s. Içduygu et al. (2008) suggest that the nation-building process in Turkey only included Turkish and Muslim subjects and excluded the rest of the population. They propose that the outsider status of the non-Muslims was the main reason for them to leave. Bali (2006: 49) argues that republican leaders, on the one hand, pressured the Jewish community to Turkify and, on the other hand, did not accept them as full citizens of the country. In parallel, Haker's (2003) interviews with members of 15 Jewish families, who experienced the Thrace incidents in 1940, demonstrate that Turkish police failed to work efficiently to stop the looting of Jewish houses.

Bali (2001: 14–15) states that the main dilemma about Turkish Jewry is that while secular Turkish state ideology considers them as equal citizens, it also suspects them as a non-Muslim religious minority. Therefore, the root of the problem is the incomplete secularization of Turkey, as the state fails to serve its citizens from different religions equally, and the loyalty is only attributed to Muslims (Bali, 2001: 16). Anti-Semitic views, in this picture, are mainly distributed by political Islamists. Bali (2001: 281) notes that Necmettin Erbakan (1926–2011), one of the founding figures of political Islam in Turkey, talked about three directions that countries could take: (a) communism; (b) Zionism; (c) countries embracing their own values and following their own national needs (Bali, 2001: 281). Erbakan defined Zionism and communism as menace diverting societies from their own needs. In this ideology, some of the prevailing anti-Semitic themes can be summarized as follows:

(1) The Greater Israel project aims to establish a Jewish state stretching from Cairo to Southern Turkey.
(2) The European Economic Community is a Jewish hoax.
(3) Zionism manipulates Turkish politics and triggers an artificial conflict between left-wing and right-wing of the political spectrum to weaken the country.

DOI: 10.1057/9781137507945.0004

(4) International Jewry control banks and constitute a malevolent imperialist force.

(5) Israel should be transferred to South America. (Bali, 2001: 284–292)

According to Bali (2001: 296), political Islam underlines the Ottoman tolerance to the Jewish community and expects Turkish Jews to be grateful and good citizens of Turkey. They do not object to the existence of the Jewish community in Turkey, although they see international Jewry as an enemy. In line with that, Islamists do not really show any understanding or appreciation of the suffering of Jews during the Second World War and at times publish accounts questioning the existence of the Holocaust (Bali, 2001: 387–411).

The political conflicts involving Israel, such as the 1967 War between Israel and Arab states, conflation of anti-communist and anti-Zionist ideologies in Turkey and publication of anti-Semitic conspiracy theories by Islamist newspapers like *Milli Gazete* also contributed to the dissemination of anti-Semitic views in Turkey (Bali 2001: 263–273). In this context, Bali (2001: 17) describes the Jewish minority as loyal Turkish citizens who do not criticize the official ideological perspective about Turkish Jewry. While acknowledging the existence of anti-Zionist movements, they deny the existence of Turkish anti-Semitism and describe a tolerant society. The Quincentennial foundation, established by Jewish and Turkish elites to celebrate Turkish tolerance for half a millenium, helped the state to balance the Greek and Armenian lobbies' negative propagation about Turkey in the United States (Bali, 2001: 308–309). Bali (2004: 25) calls the members of the Jewish community, who has good relations with Turkish state and serves to its interests, the Jews of the state, *devletin Yahudisi*. The Jews of the state act as brokers between their community and the Turkish state, and the Quincentennial foundation is a good example of that. However, they are not much trusted by the community and are seen as the state's men, incapable of representing the community's interests (Bali, 2001: 28). Despite their service to the state, they tend not to be exempted from the exclusionary attitude of the Turkish state (Bali, 2004: 25).

Brink-Danan (2011, 2012: 6), who conducted an ethnographic study with the Turkish-Jewish community, argues that Turkish Jews have to perform to be loyal patriots as well as representing a colour of the cosmopolitan, tolerant culture of Turkish society. Even though the official Turkish approach to the community is shaped by the discourse of multiculturalism, she reminds us that 'despite the idyllic official discourse

DOI: 10.1057/9781137507945.0004

of Turkish tolerance, Istanbul's Jews today gather in homes, schools, and synagogues unmarked as Jewish spaces.' Brink-Danan (2012: 88) underlines that the Turkish-Jewish community keeps a low profile as a strategy to be in tune with the secular Turkish state ideology that confines religious identity to private space: 'Turkish Jews practice a quiet cultural citizenship less threatening to a state that directly or indirectly supports a classic Turkish republican (Kemalist) ideology, in which difference is a private matter. "Jewish" Turkishness exists in small, symbolic gestures as well as in the idea that the Jews still retain a private collective that is not privy to non-Jews.' Brink-Danan (2012: 2) provides an example about the Jewish tendency to veil their identity publicly from her observation on the discussion about the use of *mezuzah*, 'a small ritual object that contains a text from Deuteronomy emphasizing the unity of God'. While *mezuzah* is meant to be placed on the doorposts visible for outsiders, there was a tendency to put it inwardly avoiding public identification as Jews. Brink-Danan (2012: 94–95) calls this a strategy to assimilate into Turkish society. In parallel, Kastoryano (1992: 267–268) underlines that the community has traditionally remained silent and hid itself from the general public in Turkey under the motto: 'in order to live happily let us live hidden'.

Like Bali (2001), Brink-Danan (2012: 57) talks about the efforts of the Quincentennial foundation to show the Jews as the tolerated other in Turkey. She mentions Shaw's (1991) work as a contribution to this discourse: 'in their zeal to tell a *good story* through educational materials, the museum, and tourism, the organizers and participants in the Quincentennial celebrations—perhaps inadvertently—conflated the terms of tolerance particular to the Ottoman and Turkish political entities towards their Jewish subjects and citizens.' Nevertheless, she concedes that 'Ottoman and Turkish Jews never lived in ghettos and were never persecuted in a wholesale manner. Ottoman political structure had a place for them as a tolerated minority; further, Jews became full citizens with the shift to a secular republic' (Brink-Danan, 2012: 34).

Alternative accounts challenge the view that Turkish state officials worked heroically to save Jews during the Second World War (see Shaw, 1991). Guttstadt (2012) suggests that the help of Turkish officers to save the Jews in Europe was only confined to exceptional cases. Baer (2013) provides documentary evidence on how the Turkish state attempted to stop any Jewish migration to Turkey and rejected reinstating citizenship to the Turkish Jews living in Germany during the Holocaust period, which meant not helping Jews to avoid being sent to death camps.

DOI: 10.1057/9781137507945.0004

Although Dönmes constitute a community completely distinct from Turkish Jewry, the anti-Semitic accounts about them also provide important evidence. Nefes (2012, 2013a, 2014a, 2015) worked on the socio-political significance of the conspiratorial rhetoric about Dönmes. Nefes shows that the political insecurities of the Turkish Republic with regards to non-Muslim minorities and the secret nature of the crypto-Jewish Dönme community facilitate the prevalence of the conspiratorial accounts in Turkish mainstream politics. To start with, the Ottoman past, an empire that collapsed due to minority independence movements, created an anxiety about minorities in Turkish political memory. The research found this suspicion about minorities and dismemberment in the content of the conspiracy theories about the Dönme community (Nefes, 2012) and in the interviews with political parties (Nefes, 2013a) and readers (Nefes, 2015). Second, the Dönmes' identity oscillates between boundaries outside and inside Turkey. They are neither Turks nor Jews, but strangers in a sociological sense. They constitute a group that could not be assimilated into Turkish society. Hence, Dönmes trigger deeper political insecurities in Turkey by representing a perfect example of the conspiratorial *hidden hand mentality*, that is, a minority that conceals its foreignness and its sinister aims against the unity of the country (Nefes, 2012, 2013a, 2014a, 2015). Parallel to Bali's (2001) and Icduygu et al's (2008) claims, Nefes' studies highlight that non-Muslim minorities were not trusted by the state ideology and this mistrust created a suitable environment for anti-Semitic rhetoric. In parallel, Baer (2004, 2006, 2010) points out that Turkish state ideology in the early republican years did not sustain the pluralism of the Ottoman period, and therefore the Dönme identity had to be seen as a 'mysterious page of history'.

These studies that draw attention to anti-Semitism in Turkey and exclusion of the Turkish Jews underline a few important points:

(a) Turkish state ideology repressed ethnic and religious identities to private space, and therefore, the Jewish identity was not openly expressed and remained hidden.

(b) Turkish Jews keep a low profile and avoid coming to public attention.

(c) Turkish citizens do not know much about the Jewish minority.

(d) The discourse about Turkish Jews is shaped by stereotypes and prejudices. Anti-Semitic rhetoric in Turkey is communicated especially by Islamist groups.

DOI: 10.1057/9781137507945.0004

(e) Although the state ideology promises equality to all citizens,
    non-Muslims are not treated the same as Muslims due to suspicions
    about their loyalty and perceiving them as outsiders.

(f) Turkish state claims that Turkish Jews are a living proof of tolerance
    and cosmopolitanism in the country.

These studies constitute an alternative perspective to the optimistic
depiction about the place of the Jewish minority in Turkey by arguing
that they are seen as outsiders, and there is suspicion about the deeds of
the community. This implies that Jews are perceived as uncanny citizens
of Turkey. That is somewhat fed by the fact that Turkish Jewry traditionally keeps a low profile, which contributes to the lack of knowledge and
triggers suspicion about the community.

c. Unexplored areas in the academic literature on
    anti-Semitism in Turkey

Various analyses (Bali, 2001, 2004; Nefes, 2012; Toktaş, 2005) adequately
list major political events that are related to Turkish Jewry. Toktaş's (2006)
interviews with Turkish Jews and Brink-Danan's (2012) ethnographic
work afford important insights with regards to the feelings of Turkish
Jewry and their perception of threat in Turkey. While Brink-Danan
(2012) presents convincing ethnographic evidence about how Jews tend
to hide their identity from the Turkish public, some of the data could be
interpreted in different ways. In one occasion, she mentions an American
rabbi's annoyance that his Turkish Jewish colleague kindly asked him not
to wear his skullcap in public. This anecdote is used as evidence of Jewish
invisibility. Although this may very well be the case, in Turkey it is illegal
to wear religious garments in public, and an Imam could get the same
warning. Moreover, Brink-Danan (2012) attributes the Jewish invisibility and the security measures in synagogues to Turkish intolerance.
It should be taken into account that the community was victimized by
terrorist attacks, organized by international Islamist groups, which could
be the reason behind their sense of insecurity. Even though the evidence
clearly reflects Jewish fear and insecurity, to what extent this is about
Turkish society and to what extent it is material also need to be looked
at, as the fear does not have to predict the level of anti-Semitism accur-
ately. Toktaş's (2006) interviews with Turkish Jews present contrasting
results, and one could argue that the community members continued
their stance of keeping a low profile and gave a politically correct version

DOI: 10.1057/9781137507945.0004

of their experience to an outsider. This data could be complemented by interviews analysing the reasons of the Turkish Jews in Israel for their emigration.

While the scholarship provides important insights, most of the studies lack an empirical focus on how Turkish people view Jews today. This research contributes to fill that lacuna by discussing the perception of Jews in general via analysing the debates surrounding a representative figure of anti-Semitism, Adolf Hitler. It examines online conversations and provides exploratory and descriptive evidence about what Turks think about Jews and how they interpret anti-Semitic themes.

Plan of the book

In the next section, Part I, the study explores the history of Turkish Jewry and anti-Semitism in Turkey with a particular focus on the republican period. It underlines important events that influenced Turkish Jewry and brought them to the general public attention. Subsequently, in Part II, the study analyses the content of the online conversation about Adolf Hitler in Ekşi Sözlük. In so doing, it affords a thorough view of people's perceptions of Hitler between 1999 and 2013. Last, in the conclusion section, the study discusses contemporary anti-Semitism in a Turkish context by reflecting on online and historical evidence. It takes a middle stance between two existing views in the scholarship about anti-Semitism in Turkey by claiming that anti-Semitic currents are not prevalent in Turkish politics while Turkish Jews have been seen as outsiders in Turkish society.

DOI: 10.1057/9781137507945.0004

1

A Brief History of Turkish Jews and Anti-Semitism

Abstract: *This chapter recounts the history of Jews and anti-Semitism in Turkey in two subsections: Turkish Jewry during the Ottoman period and the Turkish Republic. The former is a brief account about the origins of the Jewish population in Anatolia and the life of the community during the Ottoman period. The latter underlines significant socio-political changes that shaped the fate of the Jewish minority in the Turkish Republic. It discusses the treatment of Jews in important historical moments between 1923 and 2013. All in all, the chapter examines the socio-political roots of anti-Semitism in Turkey from a historical perspective and provides a background for the discussion in the next chapter.*

Nefes, Türkay Salim. *Online Anti-Semitism in Turkey.*
New York: Palgrave Macmillan, 2015.
DOI: 10.1057/9781137507945.0005.

Introduction

This section outlines significant historical events that are relevant to Turkish Jews and anti-Semitism. It should be reminded that the collection of these events does not represent the entire Jewish history in Turkey, which is far beyond the scope of this study. The intention here is to provide a brief sketch of Jewish history in Turkey. The first part of this chapter focuses on the origins of the community and Ottoman Jewry. Then, the study details the main focus of this section, the Turkish-Jewish relations during the Turkish Republic.

Jewish life in Anatolia before the establishment of the Turkish Republic

The origins of the Jewish minority in Turkey

The Jewish presence in Anatolia dates back to 4 BC according to archaeological evidence (Güleryüz, 2013). Moreover, Romaniot Jews lived 11 centuries during the rule of the Eastern Roman Empire between 300 and 1453 AD (Güleryüz, 2013). The Ottomans encountered this native Greek-speaking Jewish community in the conquered lands of Asia Minor, the Byzantine capital of Constantinople, in Greece and in some of the Balkan cities (Lewis, 1984: 120). This community followed the liturgy of the Jews of the Byzantine Empire, *Minhag Romania* (Lewis, 1984). Subsequently, immigrants from Europe, predominantly Ashkenazi Jews, arrived in the fifteenth century (Lewis, 1984). The most significant immigration wave took place after the expulsion of Jews from the Iberian Peninsula in the fifteenth century (Lewis, 1984). The Ottoman Sultan Bayazid II welcomed the expelled Jews from Spain and Portugal to settle in the Ottoman Empire, and the greatest Jewish migration to the Ottoman land took place during his rule (Lewis, 1984: 50). These Sephardic groups mainly moved to Salonika, Izmir, Edirne and other cities in the Ottoman Empire. Some members of the community established the first printing press (Güleryüz, 2012).

The Ottoman Jewry in the millet system

The Jewish minority lived under the millet system between the fifteenth and the nineteenth centuries. This system allowed religious minorities

DOI: 10.1057/9781137507945.0005

of the Ottoman Empire, namely Christians and Jews, to implement their own laws, education and authority according to their beliefs (Lewis, 1984: 126). Jews were organized around the authority of Chief Rabbi, *hahambasi*, which had almost the same status as the heads of the Greek and Armenian churches. In the millet system, although non-Muslim minorities have autonomy, they were still in a subordinate position to the Muslim ruler (Icduygu et al. 2008: 362). They had to pay extra taxes and could not become state officers. The millet system gradually degraded during the decline of the Ottoman Empire in the nineteenth century due to nationalist movements. The system was not used in the Turkish Republic, the successor to the Ottoman Empire.

Lewis (1984: 137–138) claims that while Turkish attitudes towards Jews in the Ottoman Empire were tolerant, it was not as unblemished as described by the optimistic literature on the Turkish–Jewish relationship. Lewis (1984) notes that there were sporadic resentments among the Turkish public about the perceived freedom of non-Muslims in the Ottoman Empire. Nevertheless, Lewis (1984) labels this negative attitude contemptuous rather than hostile. The reason behind this, according to Lewis (1984), was the Ottoman authorities' pragmatic perception of the migration of the community, as they perceived Jewish migration as beneficial particularly in terms of knowledge and capital brought by them, and therefore encouraged it. According to Inalcik and Quataert (1997), Jewish bankers and tax-farmers gained a predominant place in Ottoman finances and long-distance trade. Moreover, Lewis (1984) suggests that not being the major enemy of the Ottomans, Christians, they were approached with more sympathy. It should not go without mentioning that some of the hostility towards the Jewish community in the Ottoman Empire came from the Christian minority. For example, blood libel accusations were mainly spread among the Christian communities (Lewis, 1984; Shaw, 1991).

The Dönmes

A crypto-Judaic community, called Dönmes, has been influencing Turkish–Jewish relations since the late seventeenth century. The events that lead to the formation of this group began in 1665, when Sabbatai Sevi was declared by Nathan of Gaza as the expected Jewish messiah (Scholem, 1971). This messianic belief in Sevi rapidly spread among Jews (Neyzi, 2002). Sevi created a big impact in and beyond

DOI: 10.1057/9781137507945.0005

the Ottoman Empire (Nefes, 2012; Şişman, 2002, 2008). Subsequently, he was forced to convert to Islam by the Ottoman authorities (Şişman, 2008). After Sevi's conversion, there were several hundred families that followed him and converted to Islam, which composed the origins of the Dönme community (Scholem, 1971). They kept their belief in Sevi secretly and publicly pretended to be Muslims (Baer, 2004). Some Dönmes, such as Mehmed Cavid Bey, who was an important politician in the early twentieth century, played important roles in the Ottoman modernization and the Turkish Republic (Baer, 2010; Nefes, 2012, 2013b). The Dönme community lived distinct from Jews and Muslims (Baer, 2010). This was manifest in one Dönme's attempt to convert to Judaism in the 1990s: Ilgaz Zorlu wanted to retain his belief in Sevi and be a member of the Turkish Jewish community. The synagogue refused this and denied the existence of the Dönme community (Hürriyet, 2000). Şişman (2010: 16) estimates that there are currently around eighty thousand people of Dönme origin in Turkey, of which three to four thousand still follow Sevi. Although the Dönmes constitute a distinct group, the popular anti-Semitic conspiratorial rhetoric about the community sees them as hidden agents of international Jewish plots (Nefes, 2012, 2013a, 2014a, 2015). Therefore, it is important to note the existence of the Dönmes for understanding contemporary anti-Semitism in Turkey.

The Jewish community during the Turkish Republic

The Lausanne Treaty

The Treaty of Lausanne was signed in 1923 at the end of the Turkish Independence War (1919–1923) and marked the establishment of the Turkish Republic. The treaty granted that non-Muslim minorities, Armenians, Greeks and Jews, were free to use their mother tongues in education, courts and to establish institutions. In particular, the clauses 37, 38, 39, 40, 41 and 42 secured a continuation of a system akin to the millet system of the Ottoman period by enabling autonomy for the religious minorities (Bali, 1998). These rights countered the new Turkish state's attempts to create a homogenous society (Toktaş, 2005: 398). They produced enmity towards non-Muslim minorities. In response, the Jewish minority was the first non-Muslim group to opt out of article 42 that granted the freedoms (Toktaş, 2005: 398), and the other non-Muslim minorities, Armenians and Greeks, followed the Jewish minority. On 1 August 1926, Turkish Jews declared that they renounced their rights as a minority in Turkey in the following manner:

> (1) The Jews of Turkey solemnly renounce all minority rights; (2) the Government is requested to issue a decree regulating the administration of the Jewish community, the schools, and cultural and charitable institutions and to indicate the means by which to assure the existence of the community and its institutions spiritually as well as materially, similarly to indicate the possibilities of its legal security. (Linfield, 1928: 58–59)

The Turkish Jewish community leaders explained that as the Turkish state recognized the modern secular law and equality of all citizens regardless of ethnicity and religion, they did not object to renouncing the minority rights secured by the Treaty of Lausanne (Linfield, 1928). This choice was harshly criticized by the President of the American Jewish Committee for leaving the Jewish minority vulnerable to pressure by the Turkish government(Linfield, 1928). This marked a new period for the Jewish minority in Turkey.Transition from the Ottoman Empire to the Turkish Republic

Bali (2006: 43) quotes Mustafa Kemal Atatürk, the founding father of the Turkish Republic, in his definition of a Turkish citizen as not necessarily a Muslim, but someone who shares the fate of the Turkish nation: 'If the Christian and Jewish citizens who live among us today bind their fate and destiny to the Turkish nation because their conscience tells them to do so, then how can the civilized and nobly moral Turkish people consider them as strangers?' In line with that, the republican elite in the early twentieth century declared that non-Muslims were part of the Turkish nation if they met three conditions: adopting (a) Turkish language as their mother tongue, (b) Turkish culture, and (c) the ideals of Turkism (Bali, 2006). Moiz Kohen's (a Turkish nationalist Jew) ten commands for Turkish Jews summarize the expectations of Turkification:

(1) Turkify your names
(2) Speak Turkish
(3) In the synagogues read part of the prayers in Turkish
(4) Turkify your schools
(5) Send your children to public schools
(6) Interest yourself in Turkey's affairs
(7) Socialize with Turks

DOI: 10.1057/9781137507945.0005

(8) Eliminate the [Jewish] community spirit
(9) Do your particular duty in the area of the national economy
(10) Know your constitutional rights. (Bali, 2006: 44)

This meant a transition from the millet system in which non-Muslim minorities were more independent units that did not have the same rights as Muslims. Bali (2006: 48–49) adds that the republican elite did not overcome the past memories of the millet system and the negative memories of the non-Muslims' lack of collaboration with Turks during the First World War. Hence, although the elites pressured the non-Muslims to Turkify, they never embraced them as genuine, loyal and trustable citizens (Bali, 2006).

These changes had adverse effects on non-Muslim communities, particularly on Turkish Jews (Linfield, 1925). The secular law of the newly established republic led the Grand Rabbinate in Istanbul to discontinue their existing organization and limit their functions to the spiritual leadership of the community, ceasing its political and economic power (Linfield, 1925). Moreover, the government ordered that all teachers in the Jewish schools should be Turkish citizens and history and geography classes in these institutions should be taught in Turkish (Linfield, 1925: 68). It was also noteworthy that the Minister of the Interior ordered that all non-Muslims would be restricted in their travels and need permission from the ministry if they wanted to go to the further interior of the country (Linfield, 1925: 115). Furthermore, the abolition of the Caliphate in Turkey and the introduction of secular law sparked anti-Jewish feelings among some Muslim subjects, who accused the republican political elites of being Dönmes and labelled the abolition of the Caliphate a Jewish conspiracy (Linfield, 1925: 93).

The 'Citizen Speak Turkish' Campaign and Turkification policy in the 1930s

The Jewish minority continued to use the Ladino language in the early republican period. This was seen as counteractive to the Turkification of the new Turkish Republic and led to a campaign called 'Citizen Speak Turkish'—*Vatandaş Türkçe Konuş*—in 1928. This campaign was launched by university students and aimed to lead minorities to learn and use Turkish. It became very quickly popular among the masses. Some Jewish intellectuals like Abraham Galante and Moiz Kohen (Tekinalp) also supported the campaign as a chance to integrate the Jewish community

DOI: 10.1057/9781137507945.0005

into Turkish society (Toktaş, 2005). In 1934, local Jews in Izmir decided that the prayers in synagogues were to be read in Turkish (Schneiderman, 1935: 239). The Turkification of the language trend continued as Turkish newspapers in Istanbul campaigned against public use of all languages except Turkish in 1937 (Schneiderman, 1938: 493). In this year, it was reported that the Jews of Izmir had decided to speak in Turkish publicly (Schneiderman, 1938: 493).

The Turkification programme of the government was also manifest in the economic discrimination against non-Muslim minorities. For example, it was reported that in August 1930 Jewish employees of the shipping industry were discharged without prior notice in order to create job vacancies for Muslim Turks (Schneiderman, 1931: 128). In municipal elections in Istanbul in the same year, Ali Fethi Bey, leader of the opposing Liberal Republican party, was openly supported by around 240,000 members of the Greek, Armenian and Jewish minorities (Schneiderman, 1931: 39), but was defeated by the governing Republican People's Party. There was growing animosity against these minorities among the public for their support for the Liberal Republican Party (Schneiderman, 1931: 39). The decline of the Jewish community in this negative environment was discernible in one of the biggest newspaper's demand to the government to take steps to tackle the further exodus of Turkish Jews, who were described as useful citizens of the country (Schneiderman, 1931: 39).

1934 Thrace pogroms and the Jewish situation before the Second World War

There were several attacks on Jewish homes and shops in the Thrace region of Turkey in 1934 (Bali, 2008; Haker, 2003; Toktaş, 2005). Bali (2008) argues that anti-Semitic publications of the extreme rightist Cevat Rifat Atilhan were influential in mobilizing the masses against the Jewish population. Between 15,000 and 20,000 Jews fled from the region because of the events and left for Istanbul and Palestine (Toktaş, 2005). After the events, the right-wing press that allegedly provoked the events were shut down, and the Turkish state declared that anti-Semitism behind the events was not Turkish in origin, but imported from Europe (Toktaş, 2005: 402). In November 1937, Mehmet Sabri Toprak, a member of the Turkish parliament, suggested banning the admission of all foreign Jews to Turkey because of their failure to assimilate (Schneiderman, 1939: 336), and this suggestion was rejected by the parliament. The Turkish government also frustrated attempts to disseminate anti-Jewish sentiments in

DOI: 10.1057/9781137507945.0005

the country. The President Ismet Inonu criticized the policemen who had ordered 400 foreign Jews without any nationality to leave the country in around a month (Moskowitz, 1940: 373). He added that Turkish Jews were equal citizens and Turkey was proud to give asylum to prominent Jews, who had fled persecution (Moskowitz, 1940: 373). Nevertheless, various events during the Second World War afforded a different picture about the Turkish state policy.

Turkish state policy during the Second World War

There are two main views about Turkish state policy with regards to Jews during the Second World War. One underlines that Turkish diplomats helped to provide a safe passage to Jews (Shaw, 1991); the other postulates that these attempts were exceptional and the Turkish state at times endeavoured to prevent Jewish migration to Turkey (Baer, 2013). The Struma disaster supports the latter view. The disaster was the sinking of the ship *MV Struma* in the Black Sea in February 1942. The ship was carrying 778 Jewish refugees escaping from Romania to Palestine and 10 crew members (Bali, 2004). Britain pressured the Turkish state to not allow the ship to continue its journey, and Turkish officials stopped the ship (Sarıkaya, 2010). The Turkish state did not allow the passengers to land, only a few managed to land after negotiations (Bali, 2004). The ship had an engine failure, and the Turkish state officials took the boat out of the Bosporus and left it to its fate. On 24 February, a Soviet torpedo sank the ship, and, except one passenger, all on board died (Bali, 2004: 264). Another example of Turkish state policies during the Second World War is its decision not to provide arms to non-Muslim minorities in the Turkish army and allocating them to support services (Toktaş, 2005: 403). This policy was called the Incident of Reserves, which intended to isolate potentially treacherous elements and reflected the mistrust shown towards non-Muslim minorities.

Between 1942 and 1944, the Turkish state intended to tax its citizens who made fortunes during the Second World War (Nefes, 2012). It, called the Wealth Tax, was very heavy-handed on non-Muslim minorities, who were charged at much higher rates than Muslims: 'On September 12, 1943, The New York Times reported that, on the average, Greeks were assessed 152 per cent of their total property, Jews 168 per cent and Armenians 252 per cent' (Shapiro, 1948: 438). Those who could not afford the tax were sent to work camps in eastern Anatolia. Mango (2006: 1021–1022) claims that the tax reflected the impact of fascist ideology in Turkey. Turkish

DOI: 10.1057/9781137507945.0005

Jewry had to endure the economic implications of the tax, which was seen by many as an attempt to eradicate the economic power of the non-Muslim minorities by eliminating them from every field of the market (Shapiro, 1948: 437).

In contrast to these policies, Lutfu Kirdar, the Governor General of Istanbul, denounced anti-Jewish accusations by the newspaper *Cumhuriyet*, which suggested that Turkish Jews did not help in the aftermath of an earthquake disaster in the following words: 'Our Jewish fellow citizens have contributed generously and spontaneously to the relief of the population in the distressed areas. I consider it to be my duty to give them full credit for their contributions' (Schneiderman, 1941: 440). Furthermore, the Turkish government began to help to rescue Jewish refugees from the Balkans in 1944 by placing several Turkish ships at the disposal of rescue efforts (Himmelfarb, 1945: 270). Moreover, the Turkish government agreed to the passage of 5,000 children en route to Palestine and became a corridor for around 150 people per week (Himmelfarb, 1945: 270).

Emigration to Israel, multi-party democracy and the 6–7 September 1955 events

The establishment of the state of Israel led to a sharp decline in the Turkish Jewish population. The strict state control on the Jewish community was an important factor contributing to Turkish Jews' decision to leave (Franco, 1951: 314). Although small amendments were made in terms of giving more freedom of action to minority schools, allowing Turkish Jews to become officers in the Turkish Army Reserve Corps, and presenting more opportunities to Jewish citizens to hold minor position as state officers, these did not stop the decline of the community population (Franco, 1951: 314).

Turkey moved to *de facto* multi-party democracy after the first open elections in 1950, which were won by the opposing Democrat Party (DP). As the DP government reduced the censorship on marginal right-wing Islamist and nationalist political circles, these groups disseminated anti-Semitic materials, such as by the right-wing journal of *Buyuk Doğu* (Franco, 1951: 301–302). These circles also published anti-Semitic materials like *The Protocols of the Elders of Zion* and *Mein Kampf*. The anti-Semitic rhetoric triggered violence for the first time in November 1952 in the attempted assassination of the editor-in-chief of the daily *Vatan*, Ahmet Emin Yalman. Anti-Semitic circles, especially Islamists, accused

DOI: 10.1057/9781137507945.0005

him of being a Dönme and sponsored by freemasons (Modiano, 1953: 231; Nefes, 2012). The government punished the conspirators (Modiano, 1953: 231).

On 6–7 September 1955, there was a riot against the Greek minority triggered by the tension in the relations between Greece and Turkey. Events turned into xenophobic violence against all non-Muslim minorities in Istanbul (Nefes, 2012). There were around 100 injuries (Toktaş, 2005: 408). Kuyucu (2005) refers to these events as a part of the Turkish state's project of transferring economic capital from non-Muslim minorities to Turks, because the shops of the minorities were looted, and the state did not give enough compensation afterwards. Nevertheless, the anti-Semitic rhetoric was confined to the political margins of Turkish society. In events such as the Eichmann trial, Turkish public interest was favourable to the Jews, and mainstream newspapers informed their readers about Hitler's crimes and the Jewish suffering during the Second World War (Kissman, 1962: 396).

Terrorist attacks against the community

There were three terrorist attacks targeting the main synagogue in Istanbul, Neve Shalom. The first was committed by a Palestinian terrorist organization, Abu Nidal, in 1986. It killed 22 worshippers and wounded six during the Sabbath services (Fox News, 2003). In 1992, Hezbollah, the Iranian supported Shi'ite Muslim group, bombed a synagogue, but it did not cause any casualties or injuries (Fox News, 2003). The third attack was a suicide bombing on two synagogues carried out by an Al-Qaida linked Turkish group, killing 23 people and wounding 300 (BBC, 2003). Among the victims, six were Jews (BBC, 2003). Moreover, in August 2003, a Jewish dentist, Yasef Yahya, was murdered by a Turkish terrorist out of anti-Semitic convictions (Anti-defamation league, 2003). The assassins were caught in March 2004 (Gruen, 2004: 228).

Anti-Semitic bestsellers: *Mein Kampf* and the *Efendi* series

In 2005, *Mein Kampf* became a bestseller in the Turkish book market (Bali, 2009; BBC, 2005). More than 100,000 copies of the book were sold in the first two months of 2005 (Smith, 2005). Interestingly, there were popular anti-Semitic conspiracy theories about the Dönme community in the same period. Nefes (2012) and Bali (2008) mention that Soner Yalcin's (2004, 2006), a well-known journalist, *Efendi* series was

DOI: 10.1057/9781137507945.0005

a bestseller in the Turkish book market. Despite the popularity of these books, there were not prominent anti-Semitic political movements and discussions at the period.

The Gaza Flotilla Incident

In 2010, a flotilla of six ships, called 'Gaza Freedom Flotilla' was en route to Gaza to distribute humanitarian aid and construction materials. They were stopped in international waters by the Israeli army, and some of the passengers attacked boarding Israeli soldiers. Subsequently, Israeli soldiers responded by killing nine Turkish passengers on board (Booth, 2010). The United Nations and others harshly criticized the military operation in international waters (Booth and agencies, 2010). The UN report, which Turkish Foreign Minister Ahmet Davutoğlu argued to be not binding, found that Israel's naval blockade was 'imposed as a legitimate security measure in order to prevent weapons from entering Gaza by sea...' It also remarked that Israeli forces had faced an organized violent resistance and were required to use force to defend themselves. At the same time, the report criticized the military operation and use of substantial force with no final warning (BBC, 2011). The event caused diplomatic tension between Israel and Turkey, which included Turkey's expelling of the Israeli ambassador and halting military cooperation with Israel (BBC, 2011).

The Jewish minority in contemporary Turkey

The population of the Jewish community in Turkey is estimated to be around 20,000 among 70 million (Güleryüz, 2013). The strong majority of the community lives in Istanbul, but there are smaller groups living in Izmir, Adana, Ankara, Bursa, Çanakkale, Iskenderun and Kırklareli. The majority of the Jewish community is Sephardic, around 96%, and Ashkenazis are the second main component of the community. There are also approximately 80 Karaites, a separate community that denies the authority of the Chief Rabbi (Güleryüz, 2013). Some scholars mentioned that due to emigration to Israel over the years the Jewish population has gradually been decreasing (İçduygu et al., 2008; Toktaş, 2005). In October 2013, Nesim Güveniş, deputy chairman of the Association of Turkish Jews in Israel, stated that the anti-Semitism triggered by the current Turkish government's foreign policy about Israel led to the emigration of approximately 15,000 Turkish Jews to Israel (Erkuş, 2013).

DOI: 10.1057/9781137507945.0005

Conclusion

This brief historical account shows that one of the most important changes that influenced the status of the Jewish minority in Turkey was the transition from the Ottoman millet system to modern citizenship. While this transition promised *de jure* equality to Jewish citizens in Turkey, there were various occasions and facets of discrimination against the community members. This *de facto* inequality demonstrated the mistrust felt towards the community by Turkish authorities. Indeed, Ziya Gökalp, one of the early formulators of Turkish nationalism, saw shared religious background as an indispensable element of a nation (Nefes, 2013b). It could be claimed that the Turkish modern state treated the Jewish minority as an inassimilable community, who should be kept in check. It should also be stated that the Turkish state has never encouraged anti-Semitism and has not left anti-Semitic crimes unpunished. In that regard, while the Jewish community was not seen and treated as loyal native citizens, they were still under the protection of the law as equal citizens. On the one hand, anti-Semitism has never become a mainstream political ideology that mobilized masses, but existed in far-right political circles as a basic ideological component. On the other hand, continual mistrust of non-Muslim minorities secured the permanence of the prejudices and stereotypes about Jews in mainstream Turkish culture and politics, which has led to violence at times. This perspective could explain why (1) Turkish state policies intended to impede the economic growth of the community and favoured the Turkish-Muslim population, (2) the governments never made any significant attempts to tackle emigration to Israel. In summary, the Turkish state treated the Jewish community as a useful non-local group. This rationale can be seen as the continuation of the Ottoman millet system's pragmatic policy about the Jews, which involved protection of the community as a non-local, permanent and beneficial resident group.

DOI: 10.1057/9781137507945.0005

2
Analysis of an Online Discussion on Adolf Hitler

Abstract: *This chapter discusses online users' comments about Adolf Hitler in the most popular online forum website in Turkey, Ekşi Sözlük. It begins by describing the socio-political significance of Ekşi Sözlük in Turkey and outlining the structure of the website. Subsequently, the research analyses the content of the online entries about Adolf Hitler from 1999 to 2013. The data involves around 1,200 entries from 1,000 online users. It differentiates between negative/positive and moral/instrumental comments about Adolf Hitler. Furthermore, the study demonstrates what kinds of events led people to write anti-Semitic comments between 1999 and 2013.*

Nefes, Türkay Salim. *Online Anti-Semitism in Turkey.* New York: Palgrave Macmillan, 2015. DOI: 10.1057/9781137507945.0006.

Introduction

This chapter provides empirical evidence on the online perception of a very significant figure of anti-Semitism, Adolf Hitler, in Turkey. It explores the communication of anti-Semitic ideas on a popular online forum website, Ekşi Sözlük. Below, the chapter describes the website, outlines the findings and discusses their significance. The discussion complements the previous chapter's analysis that described the Turkish *de jure* acceptance of Jews as equal citizens and *de facto* practice of seeing them as outsiders.

Ekşi Sözlük: the most popular online forum in Turkey

Founded in 1999, Ekşi Sözlük is a collaborative hypertext dictionary based on the concept of websites built up on contribution (Arman, 2006). Although it is based on similar principles to Wikipedia, users do not have to write correct information about things, and most often they express their own personal feelings about the topics of their choice. According to its founder, Sedat Kapanoğlu, the general profile of Ekşi Sözlük users is 18–24 year-olds and open-minded people, as the dictionary provides freedom of expression to all views, and the users have to be tolerant (Aydemir, 2011: 362–363). In March 2015, Ekşi Sözlük came ninth among the most popular websites in Turkey, and was the most popular site acting as a forum in Turkish (alexa.com, 2015). According to Soylu (2009: 2), the website gets approximately 20,000 visits every day. In 2013, Ekşi Sözlük had 321,794 registered users, 50,071 of which were registered writers contributing to the discussions (Ekşi Sözlük, 2013a). The popularity of the website is also apparent in its successful campaigns, such as sending second-hand books to a school in the Southeast of Turkey. Sedat Kapanoğlu remarks that during the campaign more than 10,000 books were sent in three months, and the school did not have enough space to accommodate them (Aydemir, 2011: 362).

Akca (2010) underscores that Ekşi Sözlük is a new web-based public sphere that creates and fosters democratic rational-critical discourse by enabling its users to engage in all kinds of social and political debates without censor. In parallel, Doğu et al. (2012) describe the website as an informal public space and an online medium in the following manner:

> Perhaps Ekşi Sözlük can be taken both as a publishing medium and an informal public space. Approaching from the first definition, Ekşi Sözlük can be seen as a multifaceted social platform enabling its users to express their opinions without limitations of subject titles. The entries are chronologically ordered (the latest entry on the top) in this free space to provide its users to make entries considering the former texts. And it is this chronological format that gives Ekşi Sözlük its blog-like appearance. By this structure, discussions are promoted especially in up-to-date events as touched upon at the previous section. The second approach drives forward the social aspects of Ekşi Sözlük. As it is an open source for discussions and exchange of ideas, Ekşi Sözlük draws the line of an informal space. This point of view settles Ekşi Sözlük users as a community which build up a public opinion. (Doğu et al., 2012: 12)

Doğu et al. (2012: 2) claim that Ekşi Sözlük became a reproductive basis of popular culture in Turkey. They suggest that Ekşi Sözlük creates a web community that represents a broad range of classes, ideologies and groups. Providing this variety of user profiles, freedom of speech and flexibility, the website is also a rich source of cultural creation (Doğu et al., 2012: 13–14). In interviews with online users of the website, Doğu et al. (2012: 18) show that the respondents find in Ekşi Sözlük a space where they state things that cannot be declared in real life. In other words, in line with the view that the Internet non-political online forums can facilitate an exchange of contradictory political opinions (Wojcieszak and Mutz, 2009), Ekşi Sözlük affords a popular medium of free expression:

> Considering the specific conditions of Turkey, we can talk of Ekşi Sözlük as a medium for those who were unable to express their opinions in the past… Even though they are usually thought to have an apolitical view, it's those people who spiritualized the dictionary by their critical thinking. Basically, Ekşi Sözlük is the most efficient online space to express themselves among other Web 2.0 environments. In fact, Ekşi Sözlük enables its users to reflect their ideas better and more freely than the real life. (Doğu et al., 2012: 19)

In parallel, Soylu (2009: 7–8) proposes that Ekşi Sözlük's success is due to allowing its users to form its content, which facilitates presentations of multiple perspectives and informality on the website. Soylu (2009) adds that structural aspects of the website, such as its search facilities, style of administration and fostering interaction among the users, contribute to its popularity.

DOI: 10.1057/9781137507945.0006

Basic structure of Ekşi Sözlük

Aside from the general public, who can view the content of the website, there are various categories of registered users in Ekşi Sözlük. To begin with, *susers* are the users who author entries. *Moderators* limit the number of authors of the website. *Newcomers* (*çaylak*) are the users who are registered and in the process of becoming an author (Doğu et al., 2012: 3). They need to write ten entries to become authors. These entries have to be examined by *moderators* before *newcomers* become *susers*. Another category of users in the website is *registered reader* (*kayıtlı okur*). They have priorities compared to regular users, and they can rate entries as good, bad or average (Doğu et al., 2012: 4). However, they cannot use all facilities available to *susers*, such as instant messaging. *Moderators* approve newcomers' applications to become *susers*. They have the power to delete entries that they find inappropriate. *Informers* (*gammaz*) are registered *susers* who report entries they find inappropriate to *moderators*. *Praetors* are attorneys who advise the website about removing legally controversial entries (Doğu et al., 2012: 4). The last group of registered users is *hacivats*, who do spelling and grammar corrections to entries.

Ekşi Sözlük users and entries

The website provides descriptive statistical information about its users and entries. This study quotes below relevant parts of the data. Table 2.1 below summarizes the number of Ekşi Sözlük users at 3 January 2014 (Ekşi Sözlük, 2014a). The total number of registered users, 474,909, and the high proportion of *newcomers* compared to *susers* point to the ongoing popularity of the website. Moreover, there was no statistical information about *informers* and *moderators*.

TABLE 2.1   *Descriptive statistics about Ekşi Sözlük users*

User type	Number of users
Suser	54,742
Newcomer	395,681
Registered reader	70
Hacivat	3
Praetor	7
Lost	3,531
Others	20,875
Total	474,909

DOI: 10.1057/9781137507945.0006

As Table 2.2 below demonstrates, on 3 January 2014 most of the *susers* resided in Turkey (Ekşi Sözlük, 2014d). Other countries of *susers* are either Western countries or neighbouring countries like Cyprus and Russia. Considering that there are currently 54,742 *susers*, this list, including 48,423 users in total, represents the majority of the *susers*.

The gender distribution of Ekşi Sözlük users on 3 January 2014 (Ekşi Sözlük, 2014e) is 250,743 females and 101,898 males, and there is a third category called penchant with 8,822 users. This shows that the website has its own cultural jargon, as evinced by the use of a third category. Moreover, Table 2.3 below shows the distribution of all registered users of Ekşi Sözlük according to age groups on 3 January 2014 (Ekşi Sözlük, 2014f). Although intervals of age groups vary from 7 to 40 years, the data illustrates that more than half of all registered users are classified in the 18–25 age-group. However, considering the declaration by 185 users of being over 100, the reliability of the data should be approached conservatively.

TABLE 2.2   *Geographical distribution of Ekşi Sözlük users*

Location	Number of users
Turkey	45,764
United States	1071
Germany	477
Great Britain	332
The Netherlands	156
France	153
Cyprus	135
Austria	130
Canada	119
Russia	86
Total	48,423

TABLE 2.3   *Age distribution of registered Ekşi Sözlük users*

Age group	Number of users
<18	13
18–25	196,361
25–30	85,838
30–40	62,311
40–60	11,764
60–100	1,661
>100	185
Unknown	3,400

DOI: 10.1057/9781137507945.0006

Table 2.4 below outlines the number of entries and titles (Ekşi Sözlük, 2014a). It shows that Ekşi Sözlük is a vibrant online community with over 20 million entries in 15 years and with 392 entries on average per user. Moreover, the multitude of the titles, numbering over 3 million, points to a rich variety of discussion topics. to the average number of entries for each title is six, which underlines high levels of interaction in Ekşi Sözlük. Moreover, there is a steep increase of entries each year in Ekşi Sözlük from 106,131 in 2000 to 4,622,163 in 2013 (Ekşi Sözlük, 2014b). In Ekşi Sözlük, the topics of discussion are also categorized according to themes, called channels: personal relations, TV, music and science. The channels with the highest number of entries in a month-period between December 2013 and January 2014 are summarized in Table 2.5 below (Ekşi Sözlük, 2014c). Politics constitutes the most active topic of discussion. Other active channels range from sports to arts.

Table 2.6 below lists the most popular entry titles of all time as at 3 January 2014 (Ekşi Sözlük, 2014a). In line with the popular channels, the most popular titles are related to politics (Recep Tayyip Erdoğan, 28 May Taksim Gezi Park Protests), sports (Galatasaray, Fenerbahce, names of

TABLE 2.4   *Number of entries and titles in Ekşi Sözlük*

Entries and titles	Frequency
Total entries	21,078,420
Total titles	3,095,867
Entries per *suser*	392
Titles per *suser*	57
Entries per title	6

TABLE 2.5   *The most active channels in Ekşi Sözlük*

Name	Number of entries
Politics	92,564
Sports	33,766
Survey	27,615
Personal relations	15,939
TV	15,584
Music	10,211
Meta	10,151
Cinema	7,723
Technology	6,068
History	5,428

DOI: 10.1057/9781137507945.0006

TABLE 2.6   Titles with the highest numbers of entries in Ekşi Sözlük

Title name	Number of entries
Ekşi itiraf	55,761
Reading titles one under another	40,910
Recep Tayyip Erdoğan	35,480
Behzat C	24,594
Galatasaray	19,526
Fenerbahce	19,387
Ekşi Sözlük	16,818
Leyla and Mecnun	16,221
Love	16,202
28 May Taksim Gezi Park Protests	15,524

two football clubs), TV (*Behzat C* and *Leyla and Mecnun*, names of popular TV series), Ekşi Sözlük users and the website (Ekşi Sözlük, reading titles one under another), and personal relationships (Ekşi itiraf, Love).

Entries about Adolf Hitler

After providing a brief description of the structure and content of the website, the chapter explores the title entries about Hitler to afford general information about the perception of Hitler. Subsequently, it provides a deeper analysis of the most popular entry title, Adolf Hitler.

Titles containing the word Hitler

There are 697 titles that contain the word Hitler by 29 May 2013. This study categorizes these title entries as positive, negative and neutral. Positive entries are the ones in which Hitler was connoted with a positive characteristic. For example, 'thinking about the recent Israeli policy and finding Hitler right.' Negative title entries are the ones in which Hitler is depicted with a negative characteristic as in the case of 'Adolf Hitler was a liar.' Neutral title entries are any other titles that do not openly associate a negative or positive characteristic with Hitler, such as 'Adolf Hitler' (Ekşi Sözlük, 2013b). It should not go without stating that the codes are only according to literal meanings of the titles; where authors were sarcastic or meaning other things, the study might be missing the intended meaning. There are 54 positive, 57 negative and 586 neutral

DOI: 10.1057/9781137507945.0006

entries about Adolf Hitler. This demonstrates that clear sympathy or antipathy towards Hitler in the titles remains rather marginal, which points to a neutral attitude of the online users.

Table 2.7 below illustrates frequencies of associating Hitler with other political leaders. It categorizes the associations with regards to emphasis on similarity or contrast to Hitler to afford more evidence about the ways in which users related Adolf Hitler to other political leaders. Users most often, 28 times, associated Adolf Hitler with Mustafa Kemal Atatürk, the founding father of the Turkish Republic. Thirteen entries are about Joseph Stalin. The other entries are about Benito Mussolini (nine titles), George Bush (nine titles), Recep Tayyip Erdoğan (eight titles) and Ismet Inonu (six titles).

Table 2.8 below outlines the most frequently commented five titles about Hitler in Ekşi Sözlük. The title that has the highest number of comments is Adolf Hitler. Considering that the average number of entries per title in Ekşi Sözlük is 6, the title is a popular one. However, it is also much lower than the most popular entries summarized in Table 2.8, which contain between 15,500 and 55,000 entries. The other titles include comments relating Hitler to the Turkish context, such as Hitler's reasons

TABLE 2.7   *Associations of Hitler with other political leaders in title entries in Ekşi Sözlük*

Political leader	Similarity emphasis	Contrast emphasis	Others	Total
Mustafa Kemal Atatürk	12	3	13	28
Joseph Stalin	5	3	5	13
Benito Mussolini	3	1	5	9
George Bush	4	4	1	9
Recep Tayyip Erdoğan	5	3	–	8
Ismet Inonu	3	2	1	6

TABLE 2.8   *Frequently commented titles containing the word Hitler in Ekşi Sözlük*

Title	Number of comments
Adolf Hitler	1,244
Hitler's reasons for not attacking Turkey	157
Thinking about the Israeli policy and finding Hitler right	117
Hitler's contribution to the world	69
The shampoo advertisement that featured Hitler	65

DOI: 10.1057/9781137507945.0006

for not attacking Turkey. The titles tend to be neither sympathetic nor critical, but mainly relating him to Turkish context: Hitler's reasons for not attacking Turkey, the shampoo advertisement which featured Hitler. The study discusses in detail the most frequently commented title, Adolf Hitler, in the next section to afford a more comprehensive understanding of the perception of Hitler among Turkish online users.

Entries to the Adolf Hitler title

The study focuses on entries about Adolf Hitler that were posted between 8 August 1999 and 29 May 2013 in Ekşi Sözlük. The lengths of these entries range from one word to several paragraphs. In general, the entries are short paragraphs consisting of two or three sentences that summarize online users' descriptions of Adolf Hitler. During the online conversation, they did not diverge from the main discussion on Adolf Hitler, each portraying a version of him. A few sample entries are listed as follows:

> The dictator, who lost the Second World War because of lacking sufficient knowledge of history...He used radio as a propaganda machine to rule millions of people...Thank God, he did not know anything about history. Particularly, if he knew that fighting battles in many fronts would cause you to lose wars, everything would be different today.

> His rise to power in Germany is narrated by a storyline about a mafia leader's increase of power in Bertolt Brecht's play, *The Resistible Rise of Arturo Ui.*

> One should read *Mein Kampf.* Otherwise, you cannot comment on Hitler.

In total, there are 961 online users who posted the 1,244 entries under the Adolf Hitler title: 812 users commented just once, 87 users commented twice, 33 users commented thrice, 14 users commented 4 times, 6 users commented 5 times, 2 users commented 6 times, 2 users commented 7 times, 2 users commented 8 times, 2 users commented 10 times and one user commented 11 times. As the high proportion of the users who only posted once might also indicate, they tended to describe what came to their minds about Adolf Hitler, and generally did not refer to each other's entries. Hence, the entries do not contain any discussions solely between individual users. It should also be mentioned that the individual users' comments, when the user had more than one entry, did not vary from each other significantly.

DOI: 10.1057/9781137507945.0006

Coding

In line with rational choice perspective that underlines the importance of understanding people's moral and instrumentalist considerations (Boudon, 2001, 2003, 2008), this study taxonomizes online users' value-laden and instrumental/material comments. It also distinguishes between negative and positive comments. As Table 2.9 below outlines, the study investigates users' comments valuing material characteristics and acts of Hitler, such as having a high level of intelligence, being an oratory genius and being a shrewd commander. It also summarizes online users' negative comments on the material characteristics and acts of Hitler: being a bad commander, losing a war and leading his country to ruin. Moreover, the research illustrates the ways in which online users show moral appreciation of Adolf Hitler, such as valuing him as a good man fighting against evil. It also shows the entries that condemn Hitler in moral terms. For instance, many entries describe him as a mass murderer. The entries that contain anti-Semitic statements in this classification are the ones that involve moral appreciation of Adolf Hitler. As defined at the beginning of this book, anti-Semitism is the hostility towards Jews as a religious group or race, and the entries that talked about Hitler in positive moral terms are the only ones that may find his anti-Semitic views as morally acceptable and just. In this view, the rest of the codes do not contain anti-Semitic elements. For example, the entries that define Hitler as an oratory genius, unsuccessful commander or mass murderer are not categorized as anti-Semitic. This perspective implies that the entries that condemn anti-Semitism are the ones that contain moral condemnation of Hitler.

The procedure for coding was as follows: (1) I read the entries and coded any material and moral statements made about Adolf Hitler; (2) a month later, I coded the material a second time and decided on the final codes. It should not go without mentioning that approximately three days after starting the analysis the Gezi Park protests gained momentum and

TABLE 2.9   *Taxonomy of online users' entries about Adolf Hitler in Ekşi Sözlük*

	Instrumental rationale	Moral rationale
Positive	Valuing Hitler's material characteristics/acts	Moral appreciation of Hitler's characteristics/acts
Negative	Devaluing Hitler's material characteristics/acts	More condemnation of Hitler's characteristics/acts

DOI: 10.1057/9781137507945.0006

caused several entries. This chapter leaves the impact of the Gezi Park protests on the entries for a future study and focuses on the comments before the event. The material was collected on 29 May 2013. Another limitation of the study is that although it analyses valuable data from 961 online users about their views on Adolf Hitler, which corresponds to a large number of respondents, it cannot be taken as representative of the general Turkish population, because (1) the online users do not have to come from all strata of Turkish society; (2) not everyone in Turkey is knowledgeable about and interested to comment on Adolf Hitler. Moreover, analysing the perception of Hitler is not sufficient by itself to decide on overall anti-Semitism in Turkey, because anti-Semitic attitudes might be manifested via different themes, such as Zionism. Nevertheless, it investigates a big sample over the period of 14 years. Last, it should be added that the study does not focus on the neutral comments about Adolf Hitler, as they did not give sufficient evidence about the level of anti-Semitism among the online users.

As seen in Table 2.10, one entry, 'Adolf Hitler is a great example of power of individual over society', is coded as a positive instrumental comment that underlines a material achievement of Hitler. Conversely, the comment, 'a leader, but an unsuccessful one' highlights negative material characteristics and is coded accordingly. Table 2.10 also shows that the comment, '… brave leader', is taken as an appreciation of Hitler in moral terms, and the other comment that takes what Hitler did as evil as a negative moral comment. When an entry presents neither moral nor material judgements about Hitler, it is coded as neutral. For example, the comment below that describes Hitler as a fan of Sherlock Holmes stories does not indicate any positive or negative conclusions.

It was usually one code each entry, as short paragraphs tended to point to one aspect of Hitler. However, there are also double-coded entries that

TABLE 2.10   *Online users' entries about Hitler*

	Instrumental rationale	**Moral rationale**
Positive	Adolf Hitler is a great example of power of individual over society	A brave leader
Negative	A leader, but an unsuccessful one	A great example of what happens when intelligence and will is used for evil
Neutral	Hitler was an ardent fan of Sherlock Holmes stories	

DOI: 10.1057/9781137507945.0006

contain both material and moral statements. For example: '...[Adolf Hitler] was a very intelligent man, but he used his intelligence badly to develop mass-destruction methods and war tactics. I think he was an evil psychopath...' This entry contains moral condemnation and valuation of material/instrumental characteristics at the same time. Another example is the following entry: 'the whole world suffers from the fact that he could not finish the job he started...' It implies that what Adolf Hitler intended to do was morally right, even though he failed to accomplish it. By the job, s/he particularly referred to the Holocaust, as this was taken from a discussion in which a few users referred to the Nazi genocide in positive moral terms. In this sense, the entry is both negative instrumental and positive moral. There are no entries with more than two codes. The differences and similarities between single-coded and double-coded entries are discussed in detail below.

The online discussion on Adolf Hitler

Descriptive quantitative analysis

As Table 2.11 below shows, there are 655 neutral, 212 positive and 449 negative entries about Adolf Hitler. Most of the positive entries highlight instrumental/material characteristics. Among the negative remarks, the majority involve moral condemnation of Hitler, and the rest underline negative instrumental/material aspects. The online users more often stress negative aspects and characteristics of Hitler more often than his positive characteristics, as negative entries about Hitler are approximately two times more frequent than positive ones. Moral condemnation of Hitler is the great majority compared to devaluing Hitler in material/instrumental terms, and it is also much more frequent than moral appreciation of Hitler from which we could infer that online users most frequently condemned anti-Semitism rather than supporting it. In addition, the online users seem to value Hitler in terms of instrumental/

TABLE 2.11   *Frequency of coded entries in Ekşi Sözlük*

	Instrumental rationale	Moral rationale	Total
Positive	169	43	212
Negative	106	343	449
Neutral		655	

DOI: 10.1057/9781137507945.0006

material rationale more often than devaluing him, as positive instrumental remarks are more frequent than negative ones.

Some entries are double-coded. The most frequent double-coded entries are the ones that combine negative moral and positive instrumental comments. The second most frequent comments contain negative instrumental and moral statements. The other entries in a hierarchical order according to their frequencies are as follows: the entries that contain both positive instrumental and moral comments, the entries that bring together negative and positive instrumental statements, the entries that combine positive and negative moral statements and the entries with positive moral and negative instrumental points. Double-coded entries illustrate that the online users had a tendency to underline positive instrumental/material characteristics of Adolf Hitler alongside his negative moral characteristics. One of the most common claims is that Hitler was a/n oratory/army/political genius and a mass murderer at the same time. This shows a critical attitude towards anti-Semitism among the online users. It does not suggest, however, that there are no double-coded entries with anti-Semitic content: some contain positive moral and instrumental statements about Hitler.

All in all, the statistical descriptive analysis demonstrates that the anti-Semitic rhetoric in the discussion is rather marginal. Despite that, the online users tend to show appreciation of Hitler in instrumental/material terms. In order to understand the ways in which the online users commented positively and negatively about Hitler, the study engages in a more comprehensive analysis of the ways in which Hitler is depicted by the online users.

Qualitative analysis of the positive entries

Instrumental rationale

There are 169 positive instrumental comments about Hitler by 168 online users. These can be categorized under 10 themes as seen in Table 2.12 below. It should not go without saying that each entry contains at least one theme and maximum four themes.

To start with the most frequent theme, many online users describe Hitler as a successful leader and commander. The reason for not separating the words commander and leader for coding is due to the use of these words interchangeably. They value both military and political gains of Hitler and often state that Hitler should be seen as a successful leader

DOI: 10.1057/9781137507945.0006

TABLE 2.12   *Positive instrumental entry categories*

Comment theme	Frequency
Great leader/commander	110
Intelligent	51
Propaganda/oratory genius	33
Willpower	20
Contributor to science/technology	17
Improved German economy	11
Good artist/art appreciator	3
Example person	2
Contributor to the film industry	1

for creating a superpower out of economically and politically unstable Germany. There is a recurrent theme about the symbolic revenge he took on France by signing the treaty with France in the coach where the Versailles treaty between the countries had been signed at the end of the First World War. Some examples of the appraisal of his political leadership are as follows:

> He was one of the best dictators of the world, who, I believe, had the best oratory skills to influence masses.

> As a leader, he created the foundations of the German economic and technological superiority. Aside from the fact that he was a dictator, his strategic command was impressive. In 10 years, he managed to create a superpower out of the economically and politically devastated Germany. His soldiers, who had not been able to afford to buy clothes in 1933, were planning to invade Stalingrad and then invade India passing from the North of Iran and unite with Japanese to control the 2/3 of the world...

> A warrior genius...His speech was like our Ottoman military march...If he was the leader of our Turkish people, we would have beaten all others.

The second most common referred positive instrumental/material characteristic is Hitler's intelligence. As it is manifest in sample entries below, while many users see Hitler as an intelligent man, this does not necessarily stop them from denouncing him in moral terms:

> He is the evil man of the Second World War; he was a genius in fields of politics, strategy, psychology and sociology.

> ...He had a very good ability of organizing and a mind of a genius... He was a despot, who shaped aspects of everyone's life today and the world map.

> ...a great statesman, a great soldier, and a great mind but not a great man.

DOI: 10.1057/9781137507945.0006

Another common theme of the positive instrumental comments is the appreciation of Adolf Hitler's propaganda success. Nearly all these entries underline that Hitler's oratory genius is behind his political success. Some sample comments are: '...Freddy Mercury of oration...'; 'He influenced many people with his lifestyle and ability to convince...' In parallel, various comments appreciate Hitler's willpower. They note that Hitler, as an ordinary citizen and a First World War veteran, managed to fight his way to the top. They respect Hitler's career success as an achievement of his strong will. However, this does not lead them to agree with Hitler's ideology. The following comment shows this lucidly:

> His life is a dramatic story of accomplishment. He came from being no one and became a prime minister! That is a real achievement! I do not approve of what he did, but this is an entirely different topic. Think about yourself, you are reading entries and writing them as an ordinary person. If you die, only five people will know and four of them will mourn. Will they cry? I am not sure! Then, think about yourself becoming a prime minister...

Other positive instrumental entries underline economic and technological development that the online users believed Adolf Hitler led in Germany. These comments do not stop the online users from morally condemning Hitler's actions. Therefore, they are not classified as anti-Semitic entries. An example to this category is the following: 'V2 rockets, which Hitler ordered to be produced, provided the basic model of the rockets that enabled the journey to the moon... He was a murderer with so many contributions to technology.' Last, a few entries classify him as a man of art, an example person, and a contributor to film industry by his life story. These entries do not contain any moral appreciation of Hitler's ideology and anti-Semitism.

Moral rationale

There are 43 positive moral statements about Hitler. As illustrated by Table 2.13 below, these comments, a proportion of which contain clear anti-Semitic statements, can be categorized under eight themes. It should be noted that each entry contains one to three themes.

To begin with the most popular anti-Semitic theme in positive moral entries, approximately half of the positive moral comments about Hitler underline that what he did was morally right and justifiable. Half of these entries describe that Jews were exploiting Germany, and therefore Hitler was right in his genocidal policy. They see it as a successful self-defence of

DOI: 10.1057/9781137507945.0006

TABLE 2.13   *Positive moral entry categories*

Theme	Frequency
Morally right	26
Brave	7
Nationalist	7
Sympathetic man	7
Idealist	4
Stoic	4
Honest	3
Animal lover	2

Germany against its internal and external enemies. One entry compares this to the Mavi Marmara Flotilla Incident and comments that Turkey is not as brave as the Nazis in confronting Jewish power. Another entry states that the numbers of the Jewish victims of the Holocaust are exaggerated. These are the anti-Semitic entries in the entire online conversation under the title of Adolf Hitler. Some examples are as follows:

> I condemn him for each Jew he did not kill;

> Hitler was an unlucky genius, who discovered the root of evil in the world...Year 2012, we [Turks] are still passive and fearful Jewish puppets. They killed nine Turks in Mavi Marmara, and we could have not even made them to apologize! Why? Israel would stop helping us, and we would starve... All of our farming is managed by Israel...How did I come to this point as I just wanted to appreciate Hitler? He created all the industry, and we cannot even produce the Volkswagen in today's Turkey.

> In his book, *Mein Kampf*, he wrote "Jews aim to destroy the foundations of our country, and we see that they poison our youth with nudity in cinemas, bars, shops and public spaces. How could that youth protect its country? How can we ask them to die for their traditions?" He was so right...

> ...the Jewish propaganda about the genocide of 6 or 8 million people is an exaggeration, because, according to the population censuses of the period, it is impossible that there were so many Jews in Europe...

The rest of the entries appreciate Hitler as a supreme and venerable leader mostly without explaining the reasons. One entry points that elimination of the unfit is natural, and therefore what Hitler did was right: 'Hitler said mercy towards the weak is against nature, and if people around him were like him, he would have succeeded to achieve his plans and be recalled as a hero...I respect him'; 'He attempted to do the right

DOI: 10.1057/9781137507945.0006

thing with great courage... It is not a coincidence that he dodged 42 assassination attempts; he was protected by the God.'

Other positive moral comments appreciate Hitler as brave, idealist, stoic, honest and a nationalist leader. These entries, in line with the positive instrumental comments on Hitler's career jump, describe him as an ambitious person, ready to give up everything for his ideals and country. Some examples are as follows: 'A leader with guts'; 'He lived and died for his ideals. I am sorry to see that many people are happy for his death'; 'He did everything he could for his country... I wish people would learn a little bit from him'; 'Someone with such a stoic character has the right to do whatever he wants.' Other comments describe Hitler as a compassionate man: 'He opened his army to Azerbaijanis, who were maltreated by the Soviets'; 'As they would put him and his dog in flames, Hitler killed himself and his dog before Russians captured them. Believe me, he is a much better animal lover than most of you.'

Qualitative analysis of the negative entries

Instrumental rationale

There are 106 negative instrumental comments about Hitler by 106 online users. These can be categorized under seven themes as seen in Table 2.14 below. Before going further, it should be mentioned that each entry contains one to three themes.

Most of the entries describe Adolf Hitler as an unsuccessful leader/ commander. The main reason for not separating presentations of Hitler as a failed leader and commander is due to the online users' employment of these words interchangeably. The comments suggest that Hitler's political and military rule was a disaster for Germany. Some compare Hitler with Atatürk and argue that the latter was an example leader. Below are some examples:

TABLE 2.14   *Negative instrumental entry categories*

Theme	Frequency
Unsuccessful leader/commander	93
Low intelligence	28
Bad author	4
Failed in economic policy	3
Bad look	3
Bad painter	1
Bad partner	1

DOI: 10.1057/9781137507945.0006

He was an idiot. He came to power because of the ruinous consequences of the First World War in Germany. Hitler or another leader would lead Germany to destruction again. It was unavoidable... He was just a mad orator.

A person, who insisted in his book that 'elect me, and I will ruin you', and he somehow got elected.

Hitler saw the destiny of Germany as his destiny and planned his policies according to his lifetime, not further... He never envisaged Germany after the war and his death... In that respect, we could compare Hitler with Atatürk to see what a great [leader] was the latter. Atatürk did everything he could to secure the continuity of Turkish republic after his death. Hence, we are still living in this country...

Many entries that negatively commented on Hitler as a military commander tended to focus on significant military events in the Second World War. Most of them suggested that it was his grave mistake to wage a war against Russia: 'Hitler made me wonder why you would attack Russia to reach oil resources while you could get oil resources in Africa. Russia sent all its children to Stalingrad'; 'His biggest fantasy was to invade Russia, and he did not make proper plans for it. He kept attacking and frustrated his army with this strategy...' Another common negative instrumental theme claims that Hitler had a very low level of intelligence. These entries posit that Hitler's political failure is due to his low IQ: '...masses could even follow an idiot psychopath'; 'Hitler attempted to control the entire world. Surely, this was not a feasible task...A leader with low IQ'; '...His sister had mental problems and therefore executed by the Nazis. Hitler was an abnormal person just like his sister.' There are a few entries that describe him as someone whose economic policies were a failure. Others claim that Hitler was ugly, a bad painter, bad author, and bad partner.

Moral rationale

There are 343 negative moral comments about Hitler by 339 online users. These entries could be categorized under 10 headings as seen in Table 2.15 below. Each entry contains one to three themes.

Many online users condemn Hitler as a mass murderer. While doing so, they most often refer to the Holocaust. They depict Hitler as a psychopath, who caused the Second World War and loss of lives. In that regard, these are the entries that do not have any anti-Semitic tone at all. Some examples of this view are as follows: '...a murderer in Poland and beyond...This is another tragic reality...an anti-hero'; 'You can see his

DOI: 10.1057/9781137507945.0006

TABLE 2.15   *Negative moral entry categories*

Comment theme	Frequency
Mass murderer	240
Evil	108
Racist	98
Dictator	78
Egotist	11
Greedy	6
Coward	4
Liar	5
Tramp	3
Selfish	1

cruelty and how he burned Jews alive in a museum in Washington D.C.; 'My hatred towards Hitler doubled after seeing the concentration camps in Czech Republic and Poland.'

Among these claims that describe Hitler as a callous murderer, some users asserted that his cruelty gave the legitimacy needed for the establishment of the state of Israel. In parallel, some comments relate the Holocaust to the contemporary conflict in Palestine and condemn that Israel shows similar cruelty against Palestinians today. The majority of these comments came right after the Gaza Flotilla incident on 31 May 2010:

> Hitler, the murderer of millions of people, contributed a lot to the creation of the cruel country, Israel.

> If Israel is so carefree and violent today, it is because of what Hitler did in the past... I think that the entire Israel is a concentration camp of Europe, and Palestinians are paying the bill.

> ... a murderer. The entire world suffered from his cruelty... However, this cruelty does not justify what Israel is doing at the moment... Killing children in Palestine today is not different from killing children in Poland in the Second World War...

However, it should be remarked that these comments, associating Hitler with the state of Israel, constitute a minority in the discussion, and there was a strong reaction against this logic. Some examples are as follows: 'It is sickening that because of some Israeli politicians' mistakes Hitler was commemorated with respect'; 'It is contemptible to compare Hitler's violence to Israel's'; 'Hitler was evil. You should not sit on Hitler's laps while criticizing the murderer Israel.'

DOI: 10.1057/9781137507945.0006

The second most common way of condemning Adolf Hitler was associating him with evil. These comments basically refer to Hitler and label his actions as evil. Although the meaning of evil is manifest in all negative moral entries, the ones coded as evil are the comments that find it sufficient to remark that Hitler was an evil man. Some examples to this category are: '...he is the embodiment of the shadowy sides of human being, a lawful evil. I despise him'; '...if there was such a thing as evil, s/he would probable preach to his/her believers that 'if you try hard enough, you could be like Hitler'; '...Whenever I demonize something, I use him as an example.' The third most popular theme is the condemnation of Hitler as a racist person. Majority of them highlight Hitler's anti-Semitism: 'Hitler was a despicable racist, who disliked America for its Jewish and black populations'; 'Hitler made this appalling comment, which gave people another reason to hate him: "one day, you will curse me for each Jew I did not kill." '

The condemnation of Hitler as a mad dictator is another common negative moral thread: 'A dictator, whose mental and psychological problems have a continuing impact'; 'Adolf Hitler was a mad man and dictator.' Other less common entry-themes condemn Hitler's personal characteristics, such as egotism, greed, cowardice, lying and selfishness. The last type of entries describes him as a tramp. Some examples are as follows: 'Hitler did not lose the war to the United States and the Soviet Union, but to his egotism'; '...Everything was perfect, and Hitler attacked the formidable Soviet Union... He was greedy, and he paid for it'; 'He was hiding like a bug when he realized that they lost the war. He was killed in that hole'; 'This tramp's [Hitler] relationship to Atatürk was not beyond diplomatic lines.'

Double-coded entries

As Table 2.16 below illustrates, there are 89 double-coded entries in the online conversation. The majority of the double-coded entries are positive instrumental and negative moral expressions. These comments depict Hitler as a successful leader in material/instrumental terms, such a good orator, but this does not prevent them from moral condemnation of Hitler. Some examples of this type are as follows: '... a genius in politics, strategy, psychology and sociology, a respectable evil man'; '... Hitler, as an example, thought me that someone who is good at his job does not have to be a good man'; 'propaganda genius, who made the world a much worse place.'

DOI: 10.1057/9781137507945.0006

TABLE 2.16   *Frequency of double-coded entries*

	Positive instrumental	Positive moral
Negative instrumental	6	4
Negative moral	75	4

This is followed by entries mixing negative and positive instrumental comments: '...an ambitious and successful person, who was beaten by Uncle Sam.' There were also negative instrumental and positive moral comments, which attribute positive moral values to Hitler and underline his material/instrumental failure: 'everyone is suffering from his failure to succeed the meaningful job he was doing.' Last, four entries conflated negative and positive moral comments about Hitler. Some examples are as follows: 'an animal lover, human hater'; 'an evil maniac, who I started to sympathize with because of the brutality of the state of Israel.'

Conclusion

There a number of important findings of the content analysis of the online comments. First, the anti-Semitic comments come from a minority of the users. The common perception of Adolf Hitler is in line with the general global notion of seeing him as moral evil causing human suffering (Alexander, 2009). In parallel, although I did not underline it specifically in the quotations, various comments cite global media products. Users with anti-Semitic views cited *Mein Kampf* occasionally, while the others give references to Hollywood films, especially *Downfall*. Secondly, the most frequent comment category by far is moral condemnation of Hitler's ideas and acts. Thirdly, the double-coded entries show that people might appreciate certain material aspects of Hitler's life without becoming anti-Semitic, such as his career jump. Indeed, 75 entries have this kind of rationale; while condemning Hitler as an evil person, they underline that he was successful in achieving some of his goals. Fourth, tensions in the Turkish Republic's relationship with Israel increased the frequency of communication about Hitler. In particular, the Mavi Marmara Flotilla Incident generated a surge of commentaries about Adolf Hitler. In parallel to the general trend of the comments, only a minority of these entries were anti-Semitic statements that sided with Hitler because of the policy of Israel. The majority of the comments,

DOI: 10.1057/9781137507945.0006

although being very critical of Israel in the crisis, were opposed to the anti-Semitism of the minority of the users.

All in all, the data shows that anti-Semitism is not a mainstream trend in this online conversation. Nevertheless, a few online users carried anti-Semitic views, and they tended to disseminate these ideas especially soon after the Mavi Marmara Flotilla Incident. This conclusion echoes the historical discussion of the previous chapter, which showed that anti-Semitism is not a mainstream political movement in Turkey, while Turkish Jews are seen as outsiders to Turkish society. The online users predominantly condemned the Jewish suffering in the Second World War, while not showing any knowledge about the Jewish minority in Turkey. This resonates with the global moral understanding of the Nazi regime as evil without reflecting on Turkish Jewry.

DOI: 10.1057/9781137507945.0006

Discussion and Conclusion

Abstract: *The book explains anti-Semitism in the unusual Turkish context by combining online content analysis with historical event analysis. It presents fresh data by unveiling the perception of a non-Muslim minority in a secular and democratic Muslim country. Moreover, the study takes a middle stance between two existing views in the scholarship about anti-Semitism in Turkey by claiming that anti-Semitic currents are not prevalent in Turkish politics while Turkish Jewry have been seen as outsiders in Turkish society. Consequently, the Turkish view, in general, can be summarised as pragmatic indifference rather than hatred.*

Nefes, Türkay Salim. *Online Anti-Semitism in Turkey.*
New York: Palgrave Macmillan, 2015.
DOI: 10.1057/9781137507945.0007.

The discussion in the previous chapters underlines two important points: (1) anti-Semitism is not a mainstream social and political movement in Turkey; (2) Turkish Jews are seen as a foreign element in Turkish society. These findings seem to elucidate why anti-Semitic rhetoric is not prevalent and needs to be ignited by foreign crises to be heard of, as shown by both the historical and online data. In other words, Turkish Jewry are not perceived as a local threat, but come into consideration during relevant international conflicts as a suspicious non-local community.

First, anti-Semitism has not been a strong mainstream movement in the Ottoman period and the Turkish Republic. During Ottoman rule, the millet system accepted Jews as a religious minority and gave them autonomy to apply their laws and establish their own schools. Anti-Semitic events, such as blood libel, were spread rather among the Christian populations, and the Ottoman authorities took action against those events (Lewis, 1984; Shaw, 1991). The transition from the empire to the republic promised equal rights to the Jewish citizens. During this period, anti-Semitic publications and events were mainly confined to Islamist and right-wing marginals. It has never become the governmental rhetoric and most times the Turkish state punished the criminals committing anti-Semitic crimes. In parallel, the online discussion analysed by this study shows that the majority of online users condemned the moral evil associated with Adolf Hitler and anti-Semitism, and only a small minority used anti-Semitic rhetoric. These comments on Hitler were in line with Alexander's (2009) description of the Holocaust as a historically significant event representing moral evil globally.

Secondly, while anti-Semitism was not a strong current in Turkish society and politics, this has not been accompanied by inclusive policies that accept Turkish Jews as a local population. The historical discussion shows that the Ottoman and Turkish authorities have taken a rather pragmatic approach with regards to the Jewish minority. While they welcomed and encouraged the Jewish contribution to the country, they have treated the community as outsiders. During the Ottoman period, the millet system assured that they were not equal citizens to the Muslim subjects; they could not be officers and were subject to higher taxes than the Muslim majority (Lewis, 1984). The transition from the millet system to modern citizenship during the Turkish Republic represented a major change with regards to the status of the community. By law, they were

DOI: 10.1057/9781137507945.0007

accepted as equal citizens, but this did not become *de facto* practice. The community was subject to exclusionary policies, such as the Wealth Tax in 1942, and targeted in race riots in September 1955. Moreover, the Turkish state attempted to assimilate the community in the early republican period through campaigns such as 'Citizen Speak Turkish'. In line with this, the content analysis of the online forum demonstrates that tensions between the Turkish and Israeli states tend to trigger anti-Semitic rhetoric that tended to side with Hitler because of the perceived cruelty of the state of Israel.

The Turkish attitude of avoiding anti-Semitism and excluding the Turkish Jewry could be seen as a consequence of the state mistrust to non-Muslim minorities in the country. Historically, this could be traced back to the collapse of the Ottoman Empire, which was mainly due to wars against colonial powers and the independence movements of its own minorities. Indeed, the Ottoman authorities and intellectuals attempted to avoid the imminent collapse by modernizing the country and giving more rights to its minorities (Nefes, 2013b). This proved fruitless and the empire collapsed at the end of the First World War. Subsequently, Turkish state policy was oriented towards the assimilation of minorities, as they were seen as potentially dangerous. For example, the founding father of Turkish sociology, Ziya Gökalp, created a vision of Turkish nationalism that relied on assimilation of all Muslims under the Turkish identity (Nefes, 2013b). It did not include non-Muslim minorities and did not accept them as an essential component of the Turkish society. This is an important characteristic of the Turkish state policy, which promised equal opportunities to Jewish citizens but refrained from delivering it. Nevertheless, today, as the community population has gradually declined, they are not seen as an existential threat. The contemporary view is in line with the description of Brink-Danan (2012): Turkish Jews constitute a small community that need to prove their loyalty continously and represent a colour of the cosmopolitan, tolerant culture of Turkish society. Accordingly, the global anti-Semitic conspiratorial rhetoric has limited impact on Turkish society, and it is mostly the conspiracy accounts about Dönmes that are prevalent in comparison to the conspiracy theories about local Turkish Jews. The secret nature of the Dönme society enables anti-Semitic circles to accuse prominent Turkish politicians for coming from that background. This kind of paranoid anxiety is not viable for the gradually diminishing Turkish Jewish community.

DOI: 10.1057/9781137507945.0007

With regards to the main approaches about Turkish Jewry in academic literature, which either claims that Turkish society is tolerant towards Turkish Jewry (Kuyaş, 2009; Levy, 1994; Shaw, 1991; Toktaş, 2006) or proposes that Jews were not treated equal to Turkish citizens, and anti-Semitism is an everyday phenomenon in Turkey (Bali, 2001, 2004; Brink-Danan, 2012), this book's findings are in line with some arguments of the positive approach underpinning a tolerant Turkish perception of Jews. However, it should be noted that, as the analysis outlines above, Turkish Jews have never been fully accepted as full citizens. Therefore, while there might be contemporary tolerance to a shrinking Jewish minority in Turkey, it is not sufficient evidence to confirm the optimist view about tolerance. Second, the findings are partially in line with the negative view about Turkish tolerance of the Jewish minority, because the study shows that Turkish Jews are excluded from the definition of the Turkish nation. Consequently, this study proposes a middle line between two existing views about anti-Semitism in Turkey by suggesting that anti-Semitic currents are not strong in contemporary Turkey, but Turkish Jewry does not live in a truly tolerant society.

The results have implications for the literature on political communication on the Internet. To begin with, the online discussion, which includes a variety of political ideas about Adolf Hitler, presents an example of a democratic deliberation on the Internet. In that sense, the findings challenge the argument that the Internet augments political fragmentation by enabling people to engage with the political content that is in line with theirs and avoid the others (Adamic and Glance, 2005; Bimber and Davis, 2003; Himelboim et al., 2013; Iyengar and Hahn, 2009; Johnson et al., 2009; Sunstein, 2001). It is in line with Wojcieszak and Mutz's (2009) suggestion that non-political online forums can be venues for democratic deliberation. Ekşi Sözlük seems to be an ideal venue for this in Turkey by being both a non-political and popular forum website that enables the conversation of variety of views (Doğu et al., 2012; Soylu, 2009). In addition, the study contributes to the scholarship that regards the Internet as a new venue for the dissemination of racism (Adams and Roscigno, 2005; Back, 2002; Daniels, 2009a, 2009b; Douglas et al., 2005; McNamee et al., 2010; Perry and Olsson, 2009; Picca and Feagin, 2007; Steinfeldt et al., 2010; Wojcieszak, 2010). While the data is in line with this pessimistic view, it also shows the forum website as a place where racism can be challenged as described by Parker and Song (2009).

DOI: 10.1057/9781137507945.0007

It should also be noted that using rational choice perspective to analyse the content of the online conversation enabled this study to present a comprehensive analysis of people's perception of Hitler and affords a fresh theoretical perspective to the academic literature on anti-Semitism. In particular, the differentiation between moral and instrumental rationales by following Boudon's approach (1996, 2001, 2003, 2008) allows for distinguishing between anti-Semitic and other comments. For example, many online users believe that Hitler was a successful leader and commander, who managed to lead Germany with a remarkable career rise. This comment could be understood as an anti-Semitic remark that appreciates Hitler, if we do not differentiate between moral and instrumental aspects of the comments. Using the rational choice view, this study attains such differentiation. It shows that despite many online users underlining the material achievements of Hitler from an instrumental logic, they harshly condemned his anti-Semitic and racist views from a moral point of view.

Using rational choice perspective or others, future studies could expand this research by investigating (1) the entries following the Gezi Park protests; (2) other entries of the online users to delineate their political views; (3) other popular entry titles that are relevant to anti-Semitism. They could also give depth to the existing data by conducting interviews with selected users. Furthermore, as the depiction of major historical events illustrates, in order to understand Turkish anti-Semitism, one should not only explore cultural expressions about Jews but also investigate the general politics about non-Muslim minorities. These steps would help to test the results of this research and provide a more comprehensive analysis about contemporary Turkish attitudes towards the Jewish minority.

In short, this book shows that anti-Semitism is not a prevalent cultural and political phenomenon in Turkey, while Turkish Jews are seen as outsiders to Turkish society. This means that while there is *de jure* equality for Turkish Jews, the *de facto* practice is exclusionary. In that regard, Turkish Jewry is treated as a non-local resident community that needs to prove its loyalty on a constant basis. They should be ardent supporters of state policy, especially during international conflicts, and keep a low profile in public in other times. Nonetheless, this is not a comparison to European anti-Semitism, which seems to be much more historically rooted than the conjectural political interests and anxieties. In the informal and very subjective words of the author of this book, Turkish Jews'

DOI: 10.1057/9781137507945.0007

treatment could be likened to the situation when you are taking care of a neighbour's children: they are not part of the family, but they should have the same rights and be protected like one of them; in return, they have to behave and cooperate, as they do not have the credit and trust for doing otherwise like your children. That is to say, the host's view is pragmatic indifference to a potential burden rather than hatred.

DOI: 10.1057/9781137507945.0007

References

Adamic L and Glance N (2005) The political blogosphere and the 2004 U.S. election: Divided they blog. Available at: http://www.ramb.ethz.ch/CDstore/www2005-ws/workshop/wf10/AdamicGlanceBlogWWW.pdf.

Adams J and Roscigno JV (2005) White supremacists, oppositional culture and the World Wide Web. *Social Forces* 84(2): 759–778.

Akca H (2010) The Internet as a participatory medium: An analysis of the Ekşi Sözlük website as a public sphere. Unpublished Master's thesis, University of South Carolina.

Alexa.com. (2015) Top sites in Turkey. Available at: http://www.alexa.com/topsites/countries/TR.

Alexander J (2009) *Remembering the Holocaust: A Debate.* New York; Oxford: Oxford University Press.

Alkan H (2000) *500 Yillik Seruven: Belgelerle Turkiye Yahudileri I.* Ankara: Gunce Yayincilik.

Anti-defamation league (2003) 'Selected anti-Semitic incidents around the world'. Available at: http://archive.adl.org/Anti_semitism/anti-semitism_global_incidents_2003.asp.

Arman T (2006) Ekşi Sözlük: A Turkish internet phenomenon. Available at: http://www.hurriyetdailynews.com/default.aspx?pageid=438&n=eksi-sozluk-a-turkish-internet-phenomenon-2006-08-14.

Aydemir A (ed) (2011) Katilimin E-hali: Genclerin Sanal Alemi. Available at: http://ekitap.alternatifbilisim.org/files/katilimin-e-hali.pdf.

Back L (2002) Aryans reading Adorno: Cyber-culture and twenty-first-century racism. Ethnic and Racial Studies 25(4): 628–651.

Baer M (2004) The double bind of race and religion: The conversion of the Dönme to Turkish secular nationalism. Comparative *Studies in Society and History* 46(4): 678–712.

Baer M (2006) Turkish nationalism and the Dönme. In: Keiser H (ed) *Turkey Beyond Nationalism: Towards Post-Nationalist Identities.* London: Health Press, 67–73.

Baer M (2010) *The Dönme: Jewish Converts, Muslim Revolutionaries, and Secular Turks.* Stanford: Stanford University Press.

Baer M (2013) Turk and Jew in Berlin: The first Turkish migration to Germany and the Shoah. *Comparative Studies in Society and History* 55(2): 330–355.

Bali R (1998) Cumhuriyet döneminde azınlıklar politikası. *Birikim* 9(7): 80–90.

Bali R (2001) *Musa'nin Evlatlari Cumhuriyet'in Vatandaslari.* Istanbul: Iletisim Yayinlari.

Bali R (2004) *Devlet'in Yahudileri ve 'Oteki' Yahudi.* Istanbul: Iletisim Yayinlari.

Bali R (2006) The politics of Turkification during the single party period. In: Keiser H (ed) *Turkey Beyond Nationalism: Towards Post-Nationalist Identities.* London: Health Press, 43–49.

Bali R (2008) *A Scapegoat for All Seasons: Dönmes or Crypto-Jews of Turkey.* Istanbul: ISIS.

Bali R (2009) Present-day anti-Semitism in Turkey. Available at: http://jcpa.org/article/present-day-anti-semitism-in-turkey/.

BBC (2003) Film clue to Turkey Jewish attack. Available at: http://news.bbc.co.uk/1/hi/world/middle_east/3276549.stm.

BBC (2005) Hitler book bestseller in Turkey. Available at: http://news.bbc.co.uk/1/hi/world/europe/4361733.stm.

BBC (2011) Gaza flotilla: Turkey to take Israel to UN Court. Available at: http://www.bbc.co.uk/news/world-europe-14777558.

Bimber B and Davis R (2003) *Campaigning Online: The Internet in U.S. elections.* Oxford: Oxford University Press.

Booth R (2010) Gaza flotilla activists were shot in head at close range. *The Guardian,* Available at: http://www.theguardian.com/world/2010/jun/04/gaza-flotilla-activists-autopsy-results.

Booth R and agencies (2010) Gaza flotilla attack: British arrive in Turkey. The Guardian, Available at: http://www.theguardian.com/world/2010/jun/03/gaza-flotilla-attack-british-activists-return-turkey.

DOI: 10.1057/9781137507945.0008

Boudon R (1996) The 'cognitivist model': A generalized 'rational-choice model'. *Rationality and Society* 8(2): 123–150.

Boudon R (2001) *The Origin of Values*. New Brunswick, New Jersey: Transaction Publishers.

Boudon R (2003) Beyond rational choice theory. *Annual Review of Sociology* 29: 1–21.

Boudon R (2008) How can axiological feelings be explained? *International Review of Sociology: Revue Internationale de Sociologie* 18(3): 349–364.

Brink-Danan M (2009) 'I vote therefore I am': Rituals of democracy and the Turkish Chief Rabbi. *PoLAR: Political and Legal Anthropology Review* 32(1): 5–27.

Brink-Danan M (2010) Names that show time: Turkish Jews as 'strangers' and the semiotics of reclassification. *American Anthropologist* 112(3): 384–396.

Brink-Danan M (2011) Dangerous cosmopolitanism: Erasing difference in Istanbul. *Anthropological Quarterly* 84(2): 439–473.

Brink-Danan M (2012) *Jewish Life in 21st-Century Turkey: The Other Side of Tolerance*. Bloomington, Indianapolis: Indiana University Press.

Byrne DN (2008) Public discourse, community concerns, and civic engagement: Exploring black social networking traditions on BlackPlanet.com. *Journal of Computer-Mediated Communication* 13(1): 319–340.

Castells M (1997) *The Power of Identity: The Information Age: Economy, Society and Culture, vol. II*. Oxford: Blackwell.

Coleman JS (1990) *Foundations of Social Theory*. Cambridge, Mass.; London: Belknap Press of Harvard University Press.

Daniels J (2009a) *Cyber racism: White supremacy online and the new attack on civil rights*. Lanham, MD: Rowman & Littlefield.

Daniels J (2009b) Cloaked websites: Propaganda, cyber-racism and epistemology in the digital era. *New Media Society* 11(5): 659–683.

Dink Foundation (2015) Medyada nefret soylemi ve ayrimci dil Mayis-Agustos 2014 raporu. Available at: http://nefretsoylemi.org/rapor/mayıs-agustos-2014-rapor.pdf.

Doğu B, Ziraman Z and Ziraman D (2012) Web based authorship in the context of user generated content, an analysis of a Turkish web site: Ekşi Sözlük. Available at: http://www.inter-disciplinary.net/wp-content/uploads/2009/02/Doğu-paper.pdf.

Douglas KM, Mcgarty C, Bliuc A, et al. (2005) Understanding cyberhate: Social competition and social creativity in online white supremacist groups. *Social Science Computer Review* 23(1): 68–76.

DOI: 10.1057/9781137507945.0008

Ekşi Sözlük (2013a) Genel istatistikler. available at: http://Ekşi Sözlük. com/istatistik/genel-istatistikler.

Ekşi Sözlük (2013b) Adolf Hitler. Available at: https://Ekşi Sözlük.com/ adolf-hitler--38290.

Ekşi Sözlük (2014a) Genel istatistikler. Available at: https://Ekşi Sözlük. com/istatistik/genel-istatistikler.

Ekşi Sözlük (2014b) Istatistikler: Yillara gore toplam giris. Available at: https://Ekşi Sözlük.com/istatistik/yillara-gore-toplam-giris.

Ekşi Sözlük (2014c) Istatistikler: En aktif kanallar. Available at: https:// Ekşi Sözlük.com/istatistik/en-aktif-kanallar.

Ekşi Sözlük (2014d) Istatistikler: Nerede bu yazarlar. Available at: https://Ekşi Sözlük.com/istatistik/nerede-bu-yazarlar.

Ekşi Sözlük (2014e) Istatistikler: Cinslere gore dagilim. Available at: https://Ekşi Sözlük.com/istatistik/cinslere-gore-dagilim.

Ekşi Sözlük (2014f) Istatistikler: Yas gruplari. Available at: https://Ekşi Sözlük.com/istatistik/yas-gruplari.

Erkuş S (2013) Jewish youth leaving Turkey due to political strains. Hürriyet Daily News, Available at: http://www.hurriyetdailynews. com/jewish-youth-leaving-turkey-due-to-political-strains.aspx?pageI D=238&nID=56659&NewsCatID=338.

Flood A (2014) Mein Kampf becomes an ebook bestseller. The Guardian, Available at: http://www.theguardian.com/books/2014/ jan/09/mein-kampf-ebook-bestseller-adolf-hitler.

Fox News (2003) Bombings at Istanbul synagogues kill 23. Available at: http://www.foxnews.com/story/2003/11/16/bombings-at-istanbul-synagogues-kill-23/.

Franco EH (1951) Turkey. In: Fine M and Sloan J (eds) American Jewish Year Book 1951 (vol 52). New York: The American Jewish Committee, 297–304.

Galante A (1947) Turkler ve Yahudiler: Tarihi ve Siyasi Tetkik. Istanbul: Tan Matbaasi.

Garrett RK (2009) Politically motivated reinforcement seeking: Reframing the selective exposure. Journal of Communication 59(4): 676–699.

Gruen GE (2004) Turkey. In: Singer D and Grossman L (eds) American Jewish Year Book 2004 (vol 104). New York: The American Jewish Committee, 218–230.

Guttstadt C (2012) Türkiye, Yahudiler ve Holokost. Istanbul: Iletisim Yayinlari.

DOI: 10.1057/9781137507945.0008

Güleryüz NA (2012) *Bizans'tan 20. Yuzyila Turk Yahudileri*. Istanbul: Gozlem Gazetecilik Basin Yayin.

Güleryüz NA (2013) Türk Yahudileri. Available at: http://www. turkyahudileri.com/content/view/246/273/lang,tr/.

Haker E (2003) Once upon a Time Jews Lived in Kırklareli: The Story of the *Adato Family, 1800–1934*. Istanbul: The Isis Press.

Himelboim I, McCreery S and Smith M (2013) Birds of a feather tweet together: Integrating network and content analyses to examine cross-ideology exposure on Twitter. *Journal of Computer-Mediated Communication* 18(2): 154–174.

Himmelfarb M (1945) Turkey. In: Schneiderman H (ed) *American Jewish Year Book 1945 (vol 46)*. Philadelphia: The Jewish Publication Society of America, 269–270.

Hürriyet (2000) Ekim'de din degistirme davasi açacak. Available at: http://arama.hurriyet.com.tr/arsivnews.aspx?id=-170496.

Içduygu A, Toktaş Ş and Soner B (2008) The politics of population in a nation-building process: Emigration of non-Muslims from Turkey. *Ethnic and Racial Studies* 31(2): 358–389.

Ignacio EN (2005) *Building Diaspora: Filipino Cultural Community Formation on the Internet*. New Brunswick, NJ: Rutgers University Press.

Inalcik H and Quataert D (1997) *An Economic and Social History of the Ottoman Empire, vol 1, 1300–1600*. Cambridge University Press.

Iyengar S and Hahn KS (2009) Red media, blue media: Evidence of ideological selectivity in media use. *Journal of Communication* 59(1): 19–39.

Johnson TJ, Bichard SL and Zhang W (2009) Communication communities or 'cyberghettos?': A path analysis model examining factors that explain selective exposure to blogs. *Journal of Computer-Mediated Communication* 15(1): 60–82.

Kastoryano R (1992) From Millet to community: The Jews of Istanbul. In: Rodrigue A (ed) *Ottoman and Turkish Jewry: Community and Leadership*. Bloomington, Ind: Indiana University Turkish Studies, 253–277.

Kissman J (1962) Turkey. In: Fine M, Himmelfarb M (eds) *American Jewish Year Book 1962 (vol 63)*. New York: The American Jewish Committee, 390–397.

Klug B (2003) No, anti-Zionism is not anti-Semitism. *The Guardian*, Available at: http://www.guardian.co.uk/world/2003/dec/03/comment.

DOI: 10.1057/9781137507945.0008

Kuyaş A (2009) Cumhuriyet yillarinda anti-Semitizm var miydi? *Ntv Tarih* 1(2): 52–53.

Levy A (1994) *The Jews of the Ottoman Empire*. Princeton, New Jersey: Darwin Press.

Lewis B (1984) *The Jews of Islam*. Princeton, New Jersey: Princeton University Press.

Linfield HS (1925) A survey of the year 5685. In: Schneiderman H (ed) *American Jewish Year Book 1925 (vol 26)*. Philadelphia: The Jewish Publication Society of America, 21–142.

Linfield HS (1928) A survey of the year 5687. In: Schneiderman H (ed) *American Jewish Year Book 1928 (vol 29)*. Philadelphia: The Jewish Publication Society of America, 21–111.

Mango A (2006) Religion and culture in Turkey. *Middle Eastern Studies* 42(6): 997–1032.

McNamee LG, Peterson BL and Peña J (2010) A call to educate, participate, invoke and indict: Understanding the communication of online hate groups. *Communication Monographs* 77(2): 257–280.

Modiano S (1953) Turkey. In: Fine M and Sloan J (eds) *American Jewish Year Book 1953 (vol 54)*. New York: The American Jewish Committee, 291–294.

Moskowitz M (1940) Turkey. In: Scheiderman H (ed) *American Jewish Year Book 1941 (vol 41)*. Philadelphia: The Jewish Publication Society of America, 371–373.

Nakamura L (2002) *Cybertypes: Race, Ethnicity, and Identity on the Internet*. New York: Routledge.

Nefes TS (2012) The history of the social constructions of Dönmes. *Journal of Historical Sociology* 25(3): 413–439.

Nefes TS (2013a) Political parties' perceptions and uses of anti-Semitic conspiracy theories in Turkey. *The Sociological Review* 61(3): 247–264.

Nefes TS (2013b) Ziya Gökalp's adaptation of Emile Durkheim's sociology in his formulation of the modern Turkish nation. *International Sociology* 28(3): 335–350.

Nefes TS (2014a) The function of secrecy in anti-Semitic conspiracy theories: The case of Dönmes in Turkey. In: Reinkowski M and Butter M (eds) *Conspiracy Theories in the United States and the Middle East: A Comparative Approach*. New York: De Gruyter, 139–156.

Nefes TS (2014b) Rationale of conspiracy theorizing: who shot the president Chen Shui-bian? *Rationality and Society* 26(3): 373–394.

DOI: 10.1057/9781137507945.0008

Nefes TS (2015) Scrutinizing impacts of conspiracy theories on readers' political views: Anti-Semitic rhetoric in Turkey. *British Journal of Sociology* (in press).

Neyzi L (2002) Remembering to forget: Sabbateanism, national identity and subjectivity in Turkey. *Comparative Studies in Society and History* 44(1): 137–158.

Parker D and Song M (2006) New ethnicities online: Reflexive racialisation and the Internet. *Sociological Review* 54(3): 575–594.

Parmelee JH and Bichard SL (2011) *Politics and the Twitter Revolution: How Tweets Influence the Relationship between Political Leaders and the Public.* Lanham, Boulder, New York, Toronto, Plymouth: Lexington Books.

Perry B and Olsson P (2009) Cyberhate: The globalization of hate. *Information & Communications Technology Law* 18(2): 185–199.

PEW Research Centre (2015) Global attitudes project question base. Available at: http://www.pewglobal.org/question-search/?qid=834&cntIDs=@49-&stdIDs=.

Picca LH and Feagin JR (2007) *Two-Faced Racism: Whites in the Backstage and the Frontstage.* New York: Routledge.

Sarikaya M (2010) Struma'nin intikami mi? *Haberturk*, Available at: http://www.haberturk.com/yazarlar/muharrem-sarikaya/519556-strumanin-intikami-mi.

Schneiderman H (1931) Turkey. In: Schneiderman H (ed) *American Jewish Year Book 1931 (vol 32).* Philadelphia: The Jewish Publication Society of America, 128–129.

Schneiderman H (1935) Other countries. In: Schneiderman H (ed) *American Jewish Year Book 1935 (vol 36).* Philadelphia: The Jewish Publication Society of America, 238–240.

Schneiderman H (1938) Turkey. In: Schneiderman H (ed) *American Jewish Year Book 1938 (vol 39).* Philadelphia: The Jewish Publication Society of America, 493–494.

Schneiderman H (1939) Turkey. In: Schneiderman H (ed) *American Jewish Year Book 1939 (vol 40).* Philadelphia: The Jewish Publication Society of America, 336–337.

Schneiderman H (1941) Turkey. In: Schneiderman H (ed) *American Jewish Year Book 1941 (vol 42).* Philadelphia: The Jewish Publication Society of America, 440–441.

Scholem G (1971) *The Messianic Idea in Judaism and Other Essays on Jewish Spirituality.* London: Allen & Unwin.

DOI: 10.1057/9781137507945.0008

Shapiro L (1948) Turkey. In: Schneiderman H, Fine M, Spector M and Basseches M (eds) *American Jewish Year Book 1948 (vol 49)*. Philadelphia, Pennsylvania: The Jewish Publication Society of America, 436–438.

Shaw SJ (1991) *The Jews of the Ottoman Empire and the Turkish Republic*. Basingstoke: MacMillan.

Smith H (2005) Mein Kampf sales soar in Turkey. *The Guardian*, Available at: http://www.theguardian.com/world/2005/mar/29/turkey.books.

Soylu F (2009) Designing online learning communities: lessons from Ekşi Sözlük. Available at: http://www.eurodl.org/materials/contrib/2009/Firat_Soylu.pdf.

Steinfeldt J, Foltz BD, Kaladow JK, et al. (2010) Racism in the electronic age: Role of online forums in expressing racial attitudes about American Indians. *Cultural Diversity & Ethnic Minority Psychology* 16(3): 362–371.

Sunstein C (2001) *Republic.com*. Princeton and Oxford: Princeton University Press.

Şişman C (2002) Sabetaycılığın Osmanlı ve Türkiye serüveni. *Tarih ve Toplum* (223): 4–6.

Şişman C (2008) *Sabatay Sevi ve Sabataycılar: Mitler ve Gerçekler*. İstanbul: Aşina Kitaplar.

Şişman C (2010) Cortijo de Sevi: kültür mirası Sabetay Sevi'nin evi'nin geçmişi, bugünü, geleceği. *Toplumsal Tarih* 196: 14–25.

Toktaş Ş (2005) Citizenship and minorities: A historical overview of Turkey's Jewish minority. *Journal of Historical Sociology* 18(4): 394–429.

Toktaş Ş (2006) Perceptions of anti-Semitism among Turkish Jews. *Turkish Studies* 7(2): 203–223.

Turkle S (1997) *Life on the Screen: Identity in the Age of Internet*. Cambridge, MA: MIT Press.

Wojcieszak ME (2010) 'Don't talk to me': Effects of ideologically homogeneous online groups and politically dissimilar offline ties on extremism. *New Media & Society* 12(4): 637–655.

Wojcieszak ME and Mutz DC (2009) Online groups and political discourse: Do online discussion spaces facilitate exposure to political disagreement? *Journal of Communication* 59 (1): 40–56.

Yardi S and Boyd D (2010) Dynamic debates: An analysis of group polarization over time on Twitter. *Bulletin of Science Technology & Society* 30(5): 316–327.

DOI: 10.1057/9781137507945.0008

Index

AKP, 2
anti-Semitism, 2, 3, 4, 6, 8, 12,
14, 15, 16, 18, 20, 23, 27, 28,
30, 38, 39, 40, 41, 43, 48, 50,
52, 53, 54, 55
Atatürk, 21, 36, 45, 46, 48

blood libel, 7, 9, 19, 52
Boudon, 3, 38, 55

Cevat Rifat Atilhan, 23
Citizen Speak Turkish, 22, 53
conspiracy theories, 3, 6, 12, 14,
26, 53

Dönme, 14, 20, 26, 53

Ekşi Sözlük, 30, 31, 32, 33, 34,
35, 36, 37, 38

Hitler, 2, 3, 4, 6, 7, 16, 26, 30,
35, 36, 37, 38, 39, 40, 41, 42,
43, 44, 45, 46, 47, 48, 49, 52,
53, 54, 55

Israel, 2, 7, 8, 11, 12, 16, 25, 27,
28, 44, 47, 49, 53

Mavi Marmara Flotilla
Incident, 49, 50
Mein Kampf, 2, 4, 25, 26, 37,
44, 49
millet system, 18, 20, 22,
28, 52

Neve Shalom, 26

online political
communication, 4, 5, 6
Ottoman Empire, 6, 7, 8, 9, 10,
18, 19, 20, 21, 53

Palestine, 7, 8, 23, 24, 25, 47

rational choice, 3, 38, 55
Recep Tayyip Erdoğan, 34, 35,
36

Struma, 24

Taksim Gezi Park Protests,
34, 35
the Holocaust, 4, 12, 13, 40, 44,
46, 52
the Second World War, 7, 9,
12, 13, 23, 24, 26, 37, 42, 46,
47, 50
The Treaty of Lausanne, 20
Turkish anti-Semitism, 6, 55
Turkish Jews, 7, 8, 10, 12, 13, 14,
15, 18, 21, 22, 23, 24, 25, 27,
50, 52, 53, 54, 55
Turkish Republic, 6, 7, 8, 14, 18,
19, 20, 21, 22, 49
Turkish-Jewry, 2, 6, 14, 16

Wealth Tax, 11, 24

Zionism, 11, 39

BPP Professional Education
12-34 Colmore Circus
Birmingham B4 6BN
Phone: 0121 345 9843